GACE Paraprofessional
177 Assessment
Teacher Certification Exam

By: Sharon Wynne, M.S
Southern Connecticut State University

"And, while there's no reason yet to panic, I think it's only prudent that we make preparations to panic."

XAMonline, INC.
Boston

To obtain permission(s) to use the material from this work for any purpose including workshops or seminars, please submit a written request to:

XAMonline, Inc.
21 Orient Ave.
Melrose, MA 02176
Toll Free 1-800-509-4128
Email: info@xamonline.com
Web www.xamonline.com
Fax: 1-781-662-9268

Library of Congress Cataloging-in-Publication Data

Wynne, Sharon A.
 GACE Paraprofessional Assessment 177: Teacher Certification / Sharon A. Wynne. -2nd ed.
 ISBN 978-1-58197-544-4
 1.Paraprofessional   2. Study Guides.   3. GACE
 4. Teachers' Certification & Licensure.   5. Careers

Disclaimer:
The opinions expressed in this publication are the sole works of XAMonline and were created independently from the National Education Association, Educational Testing Service, or any State Department of Education, National Evaluation Systems or other testing affiliates.

Between the time of publication and printing, state specific standards as well as testing formats and website information may change that is not included in part or in whole within this product. Sample test questions are developed by XAMonline and reflect similar content as on real tests; however, they are not former tests. XAMonline assembles content that aligns with state standards but makes no claims nor guarantees teacher candidates a passing score. Numerical scores are determined by testing companies such as NES or ETS and then are compared with individual state standards. A passing score varies from state to state.

Printed in the United States of America   œ-1

GACE: Paraprofessional Assessment 177
ISBN: 978-1-58197-544-4

TEACHER CERTIFICATION STUDY GUIDE

Table of Contents

SUBAREA III.   **MATHEMATICS**

Study Tips:

1. **Some foods aid the learning process.** Foods such as milk, nuts, seeds, rice, and oats help your study efforts by releasing natural memory enhancers called CCKs (*cholecystokinin*) composed of *tryptophan*, *choline*, and *phenylalanine*. All of these chemicals enhance the neurotransmitters associated with memory. Before studying, try a light, protein-rich meal of eggs, turkey, and fish. All of these foods release the memory enhancing chemicals. The better the connections, the more you comprehend.

    Likewise, before you take a test, stick to a light snack of energy boosting and relaxing foods. A glass of milk, a piece of fruit, or some peanuts all release various memory-boosting chemicals and help you to relax and focus on the subject at hand.

2. **Learn to take great notes.** A by-product of our modern culture is that we have grown accustomed to getting our information in short doses (i.e. TV news sound bites or USA Today style newspaper articles.)

    Consequently, we've subconsciously trained ourselves to assimilate information better in neat little packages. If your notes are scrawled all over the paper, it fragments the flow of the information. Strive for clarity.

    Newspapers use a standard format to achieve clarity. Your notes can be much clearer through use of proper formatting. A very effective format is called the *Cornell Method.* Take a sheet of loose-leaf lined notebook paper and draw a line all the way down the paper about 1-2" from the left-hand edge. Draw another line across the width of the paper about 1-2" up from the bottom. Repeat this process on the reverse side of the page.

    Look at the highly effective result. You have ample room for notes, a left hand margin for special emphasis items or inserting supplementary data from the textbook, a large area at the bottom for a brief summary, and a little rectangular space for just about anything you want.

3. **Dissect the material.** Too often we focus on the details and don't gather an understanding of the concept. However, if you simply memorize only dates, places, or names, you may well miss the whole point of the subject.

    A key way to understand things is to put them in your own words. If you are working from a textbook, automatically summarize each paragraph in your mind. If you are outlining text, don't simply copy the author's words. *Rephrase* them in your own words. You remember your own thoughts and words much better than someone else's, and subconsciously tend to associate the important details to the core concepts.

4. **Turn every heading and caption in to a question.** Pull apart written material paragraph by paragraph and don't forget the captions under the illustrations.

Example: If the heading is "Stream Erosion", flip it around to read "Why do streams erode?" Then answer the questions.

If you train your mind to think in a series of questions and answers, not only will you learn more, but it also helps to lessen the test anxiety because you are used to answering questions.

5. **Read, Read, Read.** Even if you only have 10 minutes, put your notes or a book in your hand. Your mind is similar to a computer; you have to input data in order to have it processed. *By reading, you are storing data for future retrieval.* The more times you read something, the more you reinforce the storage of data.

Even if you don't fully understand something on the first pass, *your mind stores much of the material for later recall.*

6. **Create the right study atmosphere.** Our bodies respond to an inner clock called biorhythms. Burning the midnight oil works well for some people, but not everyone. If possible, set aside a particular place to study that is free of distractions. Shut off the television, cell phone, pager and exile your friends and family during your study period.

If you really are bothered by silence, try background music. Not rock, not hip-hop, not country, but classical. Light classical music at a low volume has been shown to aid in concentration. Don't pick anything with lyrics; you end up singing along. Try just about anything by Mozart, generally light and airy, it subconsciously evokes pleasant emotions and helps relax you.

7. **Limit the use of highlighters.** At best, it's difficult to read a page full of yellow, pink, blue, and green streaks. Try staring at a neon sign for a while and you'll soon see my point, the horde of colors obscure the message. A quick note, a brief dash of color, an underline, and an arrow pointing to a particular passage is much clearer than a horde of highlighted words.

8. **Budget your study time.** Although you shouldn't ignore any of the material, allocate your available study time in the same ratio that topics may appear on the test.

Testing Tips:

1. **Don't outsmart yourself.** Don't read anything into the question. Don't make an assumption that the test writer is looking for something else than what is asked. Stick to the question as written and don't read extra things into it.

2. **Read the question and all the choices** *twice* **before answering the question.** You may miss something by not carefully reading, and then re-reading both the question and the answers. If you really don't have a clue as to the right answer, leave it blank on the first time through. Go on to the other questions, as they may provide a clue as to how to answer the skipped questions. If later on, you still can't answer the skipped ones . . . *Guess.* The only penalty for guessing is that you *might* get it wrong. Only one thing is certain; if you don't put anything down, you will get it wrong!

3. **Turn the question into a statement.** Look at the way the questions are worded. The syntax of the question usually provides a clue. Does it seem more familiar as a statement rather than as a question? Does it sound strange? By turning a question into a statement, you may be able to spot if an answer sounds right, and it may also trigger memories of material you have read.

4. **Look for hidden clues.** It's actually very difficult to compose multiple-foil (choice) questions without giving away part of the answer in the options presented. In most multiple-choice questions you can often readily eliminate one or two of the potential answers. This leaves you with only two real possibilities and automatically your odds go to fifty-fifty for very little work.

5. **Trust your instincts.** For every fact that you have read, you subconsciously retain something of that knowledge. On questions that you aren't really certain about, go with your basic instincts, **your first impression on how to answer a question is usually correct.**

6. **Mark your answers directly on the test booklet.** Don't bother trying to fill in the optical scan sheet on the first pass through the test. Just be very careful not to miss-mark your answers when you eventually transcribe them to the scan sheet.

7. **Watch the clock!** You have a set amount of time to answer the questions. Don't get bogged down trying to answer a single question at the expense of 10 questions you can more readily answer

COMPETENCY 1.0   UNDERSTAND THE MEANING OF COMMON VOCABULARY WORDS AND STRATEGIES FOR DERIVING THE MEANING OF UNFAMILIAR WORDS

Skill 1.1   Identify meaning of words or phrases in context

Context clues help readers determine the meaning of words they are not familiar with. The context of a word is the sentence or sentences that surrounds the word.

Read the following sentences and attempt to determine the meanings of the words in bold print.

> The **luminosity** of the room was so incredible that there was no need for lights.

> > If there was no need for lights then one must assume that the word luminosity has something to do with giving off light. The definition of luminosity is: the emission of light.

> Jamie could not understand Joe's feelings. His mood swings made understanding him somewhat of an **enigma.**

> > The fact that he could not be understood made him somewhat of a puzzle. The definition of enigma is: a mystery or puzzle.

Familiarity with word roots (the basic elements of words) and with prefixes can also help one determine the meanings of unknown words.

Following is a partial list of roots and prefixes. It might be useful to review these.

Root	Meaning	Example
aqua	water	aqualung
astro	stars	astrology
bio	life	biology
carn	meat	carnivorous
circum	around	circumnavigate
geo	earth	geology
herb	plant	herbivorous
mal	bad	malicious
neo	new	neonatal
tele	distant	telescope

Prefix	Meaning	Example
un-	not	unnamed
re-	again	reenter
il-	not	illegible
pre-	before	preset
mis-	incorrectly	misstate
in-	not	informal
anti-	against	antiwar
de-	opposite	derail
post-	after	postwar
ir-	not	irresponsible

Word forms

Sometimes a very familiar word can appear as a different part of speech.

You may have heard that *fraud* involves a criminal misrepresentation, so when it appears as the adjective form *fraudulent* ("He was suspected of fraudulent activities") you can make an educated guess.

You probably know that something out of date is *obsolete;* therefore, when you read about "built-in *obsolescence*," you can detect the meaning of the unfamiliar word.

Practice Questions: Read the following sentences and attempt to determine the meanings of the underlined words.

1.   Farmer John got a two-horse plow and went to work. Straight <u>furrows</u> stretched out behind him.

The word <u>furrows</u> means

    (A) long cuts made by plow
    (B) vast, open fields
    (C) rows of corn
    (D) pairs of hitched horses

2.   The survivors struggled ahead, <u>shambling</u> through the terrible cold, doing their best not to fall.

The word <u>shambling</u> means

    (A) frozen in place
    (B) running
    (C) shivering uncontrollably
    (D) walking awkwardly

Answers:

1. (A) is the correct answer. The words "straight" and the expression "stretched out behind him" are your clues.

2. (D) is the correct answer. The words "ahead" and "through" are your clues.

The context for a word is the written passage that surrounds it. Sometimes the writer offers synonyms—words that have nearly the same meaning. Context clues can appear within the sentence itself, within the preceding and/or following sentence(s), or in the passage as a whole.

Sentence clues

Often, a writer will actually **define** a difficult or particularly important word for you the first time it appears in a passage. Phrases like *that is, such as, which is,* or *is called* might announce the writer's intention to give just the definition you need. Occasionally, a writer will simply use a synonym (a word that means the same thing) or near-synonym joined by the word *or.* Look at the following examples:

> The <u>credibility,</u> *that is to say the believability, of the witness was called into question by evidence of previous perjury.*
> *Nothing would <u>assuage</u> or lessen the child's grief.*

Punctuation at the sentence level is often a clue to the meaning of a word. Commas, parentheses, quotation marks and dashes tell the reader that a definition is being offered by the writer.

> *A tendency toward <u>hyperbole,</u> extravagant exaggeration, is a common flaw among persuasive writers.*

> *Political <u>apathy</u> - lack of interest - can lead to the death of the state.*

A writer might simply give an **explanation** in other words that you can understand, in the same sentence:

> *The <u>xenophobic</u> townspeople were suspicious of every foreigner.*

Writers also explain a word in terms of its opposite at the sentence level:

> *His <u>incarceration</u> was ended, and he was elated to be out of jail.*

Adjacent sentence clues

The context for a word goes beyond the sentence in which it appears. At times, the writer uses adjacent (adjoining) sentences to present an explanation or definition:

> *The 200 dollars for the car repair would have to come out of the <u>contingency</u> fund. Fortunately, Angela's father had taught her to keep some money set aside for just such emergencies.*

Analysis: The second sentence offers a clue to the definition of *contingency* as used in this sentence: "emergencies." Therefore, a fund for contingencies would be money tucked away for unforeseen and/or urgent events.

Entire passage clues

On occasion, you must look at an entire paragraph or passage to figure out the definition of a word or term. In the following paragraph, notice how the word *nostalgia* undergoes a form of extended definition throughout the selection rather than in just one sentence.

> *The word <u>nostalgia</u> links Greek words for "away from home" and "pain." If you're feeling <u>nostalgic,</u> then, you are probably in some physical distress or discomfort, suffering from a feeling of alienation and separation from love ones or loved places. <u>Nostalgia</u> is that awful feeling you remember the first time you went away to camp or spent the weekend with a friend's family—homesickness, or some condition even more painful than that. But in common use, <u>nostalgia</u> has come to have more sentimental associations. A few years back, for example, a <u>nostalgia</u> craze had to do with the 1950s. We resurrected poodle skirts and saddle shoes, built new restaurants to look like old ones, and tried to make chicken a la king just as mother probably never made it. In TV situation comedies, we recreated a pleasant world that probably never existed and relished our <u>nostalgia,</u> longing for a homey, comfortable lost time.*

Skill 1.2   Recognize synonyms and antonyms for words

Synonyms are words that have similar meanings. Sometimes, synonyms can be used to in place of another word to make a draft more appealing or descriptive. Teachers should encourage their students to utilize appropriate synonyms when drafting or revising their work to expand a written work's interest and imagery. Paper or computer thesauruses are helpful in incorporating synonyms into one's writing.

> Examples of synonyms:
> Happy – gay, joyful, ecstatic, content, cheerful
> Angry – irritated, fuming, livid, irate, annoyed
> Beautiful - gorgeous, attractive, striking

However, teachers should also alert students that sometimes one word cannot be simply replaced by another just because it was listed as a synonym. Sometimes the meaning or the connotation will vary somewhat. For example, in the sentence, "Harold was <u>angry</u> when his brother spilled finger paint on his book report," replacing "angry" with "fuming" would be a better choice than "annoyed" as the words describe the situation a little differently. As teachers work with students, they can help students expand their vocabularies so students know which synonyms to use.

Antonyms are words that have opposite meanings. Like with synonyms, thesauruses will help students identify words that are antonyms.

> Examples of antonyms:
> Sad – cheerful, delighted
> Angry - calm, content
> Beautiful – ugly, repulsive, hideous

Skill 1.3   Recognize correct use of commonly misused words (e.g., their/they're, to/too)

Students frequently encounter problems with homonyms—words that are spelled and pronounced the same as another but that have different meanings such as *mean*, a verb, "to intend"; *mean* an adjective, "unkind"; and *mean* a noun or adjective, "average." These words are actually both homonyms and homographs (written the same way). A similar phenomenon that causes trouble is heteronyms (also sometimes called heterophones), words that are spelled the same but have different pronunciations and meanings (in other words, they are homographs that differ in pronunciation or, technically, homographs that are not homophones). For example, the homographs *desert* (abandon) and *desert* (arid region) are heteronyms (pronounced differently); but *mean* (intend) and *mean* (average) are not. They are pronounced the same, or are homonyms.

Another similar occurrence in English is the capitonym, a word that is spelled the same but has different meanings when it is capitalized and may or may not have different pronunciations. Example: *polish* (to make shiny) and *Polish* (from Poland).

Some of the most troubling homonyms are those that are spelled differently but sound the same. Examples: *its* (3d person singular neuter pronoun) and *it's* ("it is"); *there, their* (3d person plural pronoun) and *they're* ("they are").

Others: *to, too, two;*

Some homonyms/homographs are particularly complicated and troubling. Fluke, for instance is a fish, a flatworm, the end parts of an anchor, the fins on a whale's tail, and a stroke of luck.

Common misused words:

Accept is a verb meaning to receive or to tolerate. **Except** is usually a preposition meaning excluding. Except is also a verb meaning to exclude.

Advice is a noun meaning recommendation. **Advise** is a verb meaning to recommend.

Affect is usually a verb meaning to influence. **Effect** is usually a noun meaning result. Effect can also be a verb meaning to bring about.

An **Allusion** is an indirect reference. An **illusion** is a misconception or false impression.

Add is a verb to mean to put together. **Ad** is a noun that is the abbreviation for the word advertisement.

Ain't is a common nonstandard contraction for the contraction aren't.

Allot is a verb meaning to distribute. **A lot** can be an adverb that means often, or to a great degree. It can also mean a large quantity.

Allowed is used here as an adjective that means permitted. **Aloud** is an adverb that means audibly.

Bare is an adjective that means naked or exposed. It can also indicate a minimum. As a noun, **bear** is a large mammal. As a verb, bear means to carry a heavy burden.

Capitol refers to a city, capitol to a building where lawmakers meet. **Capital** also refers to wealth or resources.

A **chord** is a noun that refers to a group of musical notes. **Cord** is a noun meaning rope or a long electrical line.

Compliment is a noun meaning a praising or flattering remark. **Complement** is a noun that means something that completes or makes perfect.

Climactic is derived from climax, the point of greatest intensity in a series or progression of events. **Climatic** is derived from climate; it refers to meteorological conditions.

Discreet is an adjective that means tactful or diplomatic; **discrete** is an adjective that means separate or distinct.

Dye is a noun or verb used to indicate artificially coloring something. **Die** is a verb that means to pass away. Die is also a noun that means a cube-shaped game piece.

Effect is a noun that means outcome. **Affect** is a verb that means to act or produce an effect on.

Elicit is a verb meaning to bring out or to evoke. **Illicit** is an adjective meaning unlawful

Emigrate means to leave one country or region to settle in another. **Immigrate** means to enter another country and reside there.

Hoard is a verb that means to accumulate or store up. **Horde** is a large group. **Lead** is a verb that means to guide or serve as the head of. It is also a noun that is a type of metal.

Medal is a noun that means an award that is strung round the neck. **Meddle** is a verb that means to involve oneself in a matter without right or invitation. **Metal** is an element such as silver or gold. **Mettle** is a noun meaning toughness or guts.

Morning is a noun indicating the time between midnight and midday. **Mourning** is a verb or noun pertaining to the period of grieving after a death.

Past is a noun meaning a time before now (past, present and future). **Passed** is past tense of the verb "to pass."

Piece is a noun meaning a portion. **Peace** is a noun meaning the opposite of war.

Peak is a noun meaning the tip or height to reach the highest point. **Peek** is a verb that means to take a brief look. **Pique** is a verb meaning to incite or raise interest.

Principal is a noun meaning the head of a school or an organization or a sum of money. **Principle** is a noun meaning a basic truth or law.

Rite is a noun meaning a special ceremony. **Right** is an adjective meaning correct or direction. **Write** is a verb meaning to compose in writing.

Than is a conjunction used in comparisons; **then** is an adverb denoting time. That pizza is more <u>than</u> I can eat. Tom laughed, and <u>then</u> we recognized him.

Than is used to compare; both words have the letter a in them.

Then tells when; both are spelled the same, except for the first letter.

There is an adverb specifying place; it is also an expletive. Adverb: Sylvia is lying <u>there</u> unconscious. Expletive: <u>There</u> are two plums left. **Their** is a possessive pronoun. **They're** is a contraction of they are. Fred and Jane finally washed <u>their</u> car. <u>They're</u> later than usual today.

To is a preposition; **too** is an adverb; **two** is a number.

Your is a possessive pronoun; **you're** is a contraction of you are.

To effectively teach language, it is necessary to understand that, as human beings acquire language, they realize that words have denotative and connotative meanings. Generally, denotative words point to things and connotative words deal with mental suggestions that the words convey. The word skunk has a denotative meaning if the speaker can point to the actual animal as he speaks the word and intends the word to identify the animal. Skunk has connotative meaning depending upon the tone of delivery, the socially acceptable attitudes about the animal, and the speaker's personal feelings about the animal.

Problem Phrases

Correct	Incorrect
Supposed to	Suppose to
Used to	Use to
Toward	Towards
Anyway	Anyways
Couldn't care less	Could care less
For all intents and purposes	For all intensive purposes
Come to see me	Come and see me
En route	In route
Regardless	Irregardless
Second, Third	Secondly, Thirdly

Other confusing words

Lie is an intransitive verb meaning to recline or rest on a surface. Its principal parts are lie, lay, lain. **Lay** is a transitive verb meaning to put or place. Its principal parts are lay, laid.

> Birds lay eggs.
> I lie down for bed around 10 PM.

Set is a transitive verb meaning to put or to place. Its principal parts are set, set, set. **Sit** is an intransitive verb meaning to be seated. Its principal parts are sit, sat, sat.

> I set my backpack down near the front door.
> They sat in the park until the sun went down.

Among is a preposition to be used with three or more items. **Between** is to be used with two items.

> Between you and me, I cannot tell the difference among those three Johnson sisters.

As is a subordinating conjunction used to introduce a subordinating clause; **like** is a preposition and is followed by a noun or a noun phrase.

> As I walked to the lab, I realized that the recent experiment findings were much like those we found last year.

Can is a verb that means to be able. **May** is a verb that means to have permission. They are only interchangeable in cases of possibility.

> I can light 250 pounds.
> May I go to Alex's house?

COMPETENCY 2.0   UNDERSTAND HOW TO INTERPRET AND ANALYZE A WIDE RANGE OF TEXTS

Skill 2.1   Identify the main idea of a passage

The main idea of a passage or paragraph is the basic message, idea, point concept, or meaning that the author wants to convey to you, the reader. Understanding the main idea of a passage or paragraph is the key to understanding the more subtle components of the author's message. The main idea is what is being said about a topic or subject. Once you have identified the basic message, you will have an easier time answering other questions that test critical skills.

Main ideas are either *stated* or *implied*. A *stated main idea* is explicit: it is directly expressed in a sentence or two in the paragraph or passage. An *implied main idea* is suggested by the overall reading selection. In the first case, you need not pull information from various points in the paragraph or passage in order to form the main idea because it is already stated by the author. If a main idea is implied, however, you must formulate, in your own words, a main idea statement by condensing the overall message contained in the material itself.

Practice Question: Read the following passage and select an answer

Sometimes too much of a good thing can become a very bad thing indeed. In an earnest attempt to consume a healthy diet, dietary supplement enthusiasts have been known to overdose. Vitamin C, for example, long thought to help people ward off cold viruses, is currently being studied for its possible role in warding off cancer and other disease that cases tissue degeneration. Unfortunately, an overdose of vitamin C – more than 10,000 mg – on a daily basis can cause nausea and diarrhea. Calcium supplements, commonly taken by women, are helpful in warding off osteoporosis. More than just a few grams a day, however, can lead to stomach upset and even kidney and bladder stones. Niacin, proven useful in reducing cholesterol levels, can be dangerous in large doses to those who suffer from heart problems, asthma or ulcers.

The main idea expressed in this paragraph is:

    A.   supplements taken in excess can be a bad thing indeed
    B.   dietary supplement enthusiasts have been known to overdose
    C.   vitamins can cause nausea, diarrhea, and kidney or bladder stones
    D.   people who take supplements are preoccupied with their health

Answer: Answer A is a paraphrase of the first sentence and provides a general framework for the rest of the paragraph: Excess supplement intake is bad. The rest of the paragraph discusses the consequences of taking too many vitamins. Options B and C refer to major details, and Option D introduces the idea of preoccupation, which is not included in this paragraph.

Skill 2.2   Recognize supporting ideas in a passage

Supporting details are examples, facts, ideas, illustrations, cases and anecdotes used by a writer to explain, expand on, and develop the more general main idea. A writer's choice of supporting materials is determined by the nature of the topic being covered. Supporting details are specifics that relate directly to the main idea. Writers select and shape material according to their purposes. An advertisement writer seeking to persuade the reader to buy a particular running shoe, for instance, will emphasize only the positive characteristics of the shoe for advertisement copy. A columnist for a running magazine, on the other hand, might list the good and bad points about the same shoe in an article recommending appropriate shoes for different kind of runners. Both major details (those that directly support the main idea), and minor details (those that provide interesting, but not always essential, information) help create a well-written and fluid passage.

In the following paragraph, the sentences in **bold print** provide a skeleton of a paragraph on the benefits of recycling. The sentences in bold are generalizations that by themselves do not explain the need to recycle. The sentences in *italics* add details to SHOW the general points in bold. Notice how the supporting details help you understand the necessity for recycling.

While one day recycling may become mandatory in all states, right now it is voluntary in many communities. *Those of us who participate in recycling are amazed by how much material is recycled.* **For many communities, the blue-box recycling program has had an immediate effect.** *By just recycling glass, aluminum cans, and plastic bottles, we have reduced the volume of disposable trash by one third, thus extending the useful life of local landfills by over a decade. Imagine the difference if those dramatic results were achieved nationwide.* **The amount of reusable items we thoughtlessly dispose of is staggering.** *For example, Americans dispose of enough steel everyday to supply Detroit car manufacturers for three months. Additionally, we dispose of enough aluminum annually to rebuild the nation's air fleet. These statistics, available from the Environmental Protection Agency (EPA), should encourage all of us to watch what we throw away.* **Clearly, recycling in our homes and in our communities directly improves the environment.**

Notice how the author's supporting examples enhance the message of the paragraph and relate to the author's thesis noted above. If you only read the bold-face sentences, you have a glimpse at the topic. This paragraph, however, is developed through numerous details creating specific images: *reduced the volume of disposable trash by one-third; extended the useful life of local landfills by over a decade; enough steel everyday to supply Detroit car manufacturers for three months; enough aluminum to rebuild the nation's air fleet.* If the writer had merely written a few general sentences, as those shown in bold face, you would not fully understand the vast amount of trash involved in recycling or the positive results of current recycling efforts.

Skill 2.3   Draw inferences and conclusions from directly stated content

An **inference** is sometimes called an "educated guess" because it requires that you go beyond the strictly obvious to create additional meaning by taking the text one logical step further. Inferences and conclusions are based on the content of the passage – that is, on what the passage says or how the writer says it – and are derived by reasoning.

Inference is an essential and automatic component of most reading. For example, in making educated guesses about the meaning of unknown words, the author's main idea or whether he or she is writing with a bias. Such is the essence of inference: you use your own ability to reason in order to figure out what the writer implies. As a reader, then, you must often logically extend meaning that is only implied.

Consider the following example. Assume you are an employer, and you are reading over the letters of reference submitted by a prospective employee for the position of clerk/typist in your real estate office. The position requires the applicant to be neat, careful, trustworthy, and punctual. You come across this letter of reference submitted by an applicant:

To whom it may concern,

Todd Finley has asked me to write a letter of reference for him. I am well qualified to do so because he worked for me for three months last year. His duties included answering the phone, greeting the public, and producing some simple memos and notices on the computer. Although Todd initially had few computer skills and little knowledge of telephone etiquette, he did acquire some during his stay with us. Todd's manner of speaking, both on the telephone and with the clients who came to my establishment, could be described as casual. He was particularly effective when communicating with peers. Please contact me by telephone if you wish to have further information about my experience.

Here the writer implies, rather than openly states, the main idea. This letter calls attention to itself because there's a problem with its tone. A truly positive letter would say something like "I have distinct honor to recommend Todd Finley." Here, however, the letter simply verifies that Todd worked in the office. Second, the praise is obviously lukewarm. For example, the writer says that Todd "was particularly effective when communicating with peers." An educated guess translates that statement into a nice way of saying Todd was not serious about his communication with clients.

In order to draw **inferences** and make **conclusions**, a reader must use prior knowledge and apply it to the current situation. A conclusion or inference is never stated. You must rely on your common sense.

Practice Questions: Read the following passages and select an answer

1.   The Smith family waited patiently around carousel number 7 for their luggage to arrive. They were exhausted after their 5 hour trip and were anxious to get to their hotel. After about an hour, they realized that they no longer recognized any of the other passengers' faces. Mrs. Smith asked the person who appeared to be in charge if they were at the right carousel. The man replied, "Yes, this is it, but we finished unloading that baggage almost half an hour ago."

From the man's response we can infer that:
(A) The Smiths were ready to go to their hotel.
(B) The Smith's luggage was lost.
(C) The man had their luggage.
(D) They were at the wrong carousel.

2.   Tim Sullivan had just turned 15. As a birthday present, his parents had given him a guitar and a certificate for 10 guitar lessons. He had always shown a love of music and a desire to learn an instrument. Tim began his lessons and before long, he was making up his own songs. At the music studio, Tim met Josh, who played the piano and Roger, whose instrument was the saxophone. They all shared the same dream, to start a band and each was praised by his teacher as having real talent.

From this passage one can infer that
(A) Tim, Roger & Josh are going to start their own band.
(B) Tim is going to give up his guitar lessons.
(C) Tim, Josh & Roger will no longer be friends.
(D) Josh & Roger are going to start their own band.

Answers:

1. Since the Smiths were still waiting for their luggage, we know that they were not yet ready to go to their hotel. From the man's response, we know that they were not at the wrong carousel and that he did not have their luggage. Therefore, though not directly stated, it appears that their luggage was lost. Choice (B) is the correct answer.

2. (A) is the correct choice. Given the facts that Tim wanted to be a musician and start his own band, after meeting others who shared the same dreams, we can infer that they joined together in an attempt to make their dreams become a reality.

Skill 2.4   Recognize cause-and-effect relationships in a passage

A cause is the necessary source of a particular outcome. If a writer were addressing the question "How will the new tax laws affect small businesses?" or "Why has there been such political unrest in Somalia?" he or she would use cause and effect as an organizational pattern to structure their response. In the first case, the writer would emphasize effects of the tax legislation as they apply to owners of small businesses. In the second, they would focus on causes for the current political situation in Somalia.

Some word clues that identify a cause-effect passage are: accordingly, as a result, therefore, because, consequently, hence, in short, thus, then, due to and so on.

Sample passage:
Simply put, inflation is an increase in price levels. It happens when a government prints more currency than is already in circulation, and there is, consequently, additional money available for the same amount of good or services. There might be multiple reasons for a government to crank up the printing presses. A war, for instance, could cause an immediate need for steel. A national disaster might create a sudden need for social services. To get the money it needs, a government can raise taxes, borrow, or print more currency. However, raising taxes and borrowing are not always plausible options.

Analysis: The paragraph starts with a definition and proceeds to examine a causal chain. The words *consequently, reasons* and *cause* provide the clues.

Explicit Cause and Effect

General Hooker failed to anticipate General Lee's bold flanking maneuver. As a result, Hooker's army was nearly routed by a smaller force.

Mindy forgot to bring the lunch her father had packed for her. Consequently, she had to borrow money from her friends at school during lunch period.

Implicit Cause and Effect

The engine in Lisa's airplane began to sputter. She quickly looked below for a field in which to land.

Luther ate the creamed shrimp that had been sitting in the sun for hours. Later that night, he was so sick he had to be rushed to the hospital.

Skill 2.5   Distinguish between fact and opinion in written texts

Facts are statements that are verifiable. Opinions are statements that must be supported in order to be accepted such as beliefs, values, judgments or feelings. Facts are objective statements used to support subjective opinions. For example, "Jane is a bad girl" is an opinion. However, "Jane hit her sister with a baseball bat" is a *fact* upon which the opinion is based. Judgments are opinions—decisions or declarations based on observation or reasoning that express approval or disapproval. Facts report what has happened or exists and come from observation, measurement, or calculation. Facts can be tested and verified whereas opinions and judgments cannot. They can only be supported with facts.

Most statements cannot be so clearly distinguished. "I believe that Jane is a bad girl" is a fact. The speaker knows what he/she believes. However, it obviously includes a judgment that could be disputed by another person who might believe otherwise. Judgments are not usually so firm. They are, rather, plausible opinions that provoke thought or lead to factual development.

Joe DiMaggio, a Yankees' center-fielder, was replaced by Mickey Mantle in 1952.

This is a fact. If necessary, evidence can be produced to support this.

First year players are more ambitious than seasoned players.
This is an opinion. There is no proof to support that everyone feels this way.

Practice Questions: Decide if the statement is fact or opinion

1. The Inca were a group of Indians who ruled an empire in South America.

   (A) fact
   (B) opinion

2. The Inca were clever.

   (A) fact
   (B) opinion

3. The Inca built very complex systems of bridges.

   (A) fact
   (B) opinion

Answers:

1. (A) is the correct answer. Research can prove this to be true.
2. (B) is the correct answer. It is doubtful that all people who have studied the Inca agree with this statement. Therefore, no proof is available.
3. (A) is the correct answer. As with question number one, research can prove this to be true.

Skill 2.6   Identify literary elements (e.g., character, setting, plot, climax)

Imagery can be described as a word or sequence of words that refers to any sensory experience—that is, anything that can be seen, tasted, smelled, heard, or felt on the skin or fingers. While writers of prose may also use these devices, it is most distinctive of poetry. The poet intends to make an experience available to the reader. In order to do that, he/she must appeal to one of the senses. The most-often-used one, of course, is the visual sense. The poet will deliberately paint a scene in such a way that the reader can see it. However, the purpose is not simply to stir the visceral feeling but also to stir the emotions. A good example is *The Piercing Chill* by Taniguchi Buson (1715-1783):

> The piercing chill I feel:
> My dead wife's comb, in our bedroom,
>   Under my heel . . .

In only a few short words, the reader can feel many things: the shock that might come from touching the corpse, a literal sense of death, the contrast between her death and the memories he has of her when she was alive. Imagery might be defined as speaking of the abstract in concrete terms, a powerful device in the hands of a skillful poet.

A **symbol** is an object or action that can be observed with the senses in addition to its suggesting many other things. The lion is a symbol of courage; the cross a symbol of Christianity; the swastika a symbol of Nazi Germany. These can almost be defined as metaphors because society pretty much agrees on the one-to-one meaning of them. Symbols used in literature are usually of a different sort. They tend to be private and personal; their significance is only evident in the context of the work where they are used. A good example is the huge pair of spectacles on a sign board in Fitzgerald's *The Great Gatsby*. They are interesting as a part of the landscape, but they also symbolize divine myopia. A symbol can certainly have more than one meaning, and the meaning may be as personal as the memories and experiences of the particular reader. In analyzing a poem or a story, it's important to identify the symbols and their possible meanings.

Looking for symbols is often challenging, especially for novice poetry readers. However, these suggestions may be useful: First, pick out all the references to concrete objects such as a newspaper, black cats, etc. Note any that the poet emphasizes by describing in detail, by repeating, or by placing at the very beginning or ending of a poem. Ask: what is the poem about? What does it add up to? Paraphrase the poem and determine whether or not the meaning depends upon certain concrete objects. Then ponder what the concrete object symbolizes in this particular poem. Look for a character with the name of a prophet who does little but utter prophecy or a trio of women who resemble the Three Fates. A symbol may be a part of a person's body such as the eye of the murder victim in Poe's story *The Tell-Tale Heart* or a look, a voice, or a mannerism.

Some things a symbol is not: an abstraction such as truth, death, and love; in narrative, a well-developed character who is not at all mysterious; the second term in a metaphor. In Emily Dickenson's *The Lightning Is a Yellow Fork*, the symbol is the lightning, not the fork.

An **allusion** is very like a symbol, and the two sometimes tend to run together. An allusion is defined by Merriam Webster's *Encyclopedia of Literature* as "an implied reference to a person, event, thing, or a part of another text." Allusions are based on the assumption that there is a common body of knowledge shared by poet and reader and that a reference to that body of knowledge will be immediately understood. Allusions to the Bible and classical mythology are common in western literature on the assumption that they will be immediately understood. The use of allusion is a sort of shortcut for poets. They can use an economy of words and count on meaning to come from the reader's own experience.

Tempo

In drama, interpretation of dialogue must be connected to motivation and detail. During this time, the director is also concerned with pace and seeks a variation of tempo. If the overall pace is too slow, then the action becomes dull and dragging. If the overall pace is too fast, then the audience will not be able to understand what is going on, for they are being hit with too much information to process.

Story Elements

Most works of fiction contain a common set of elements that make them come alive to readers. In a way, even though writers do not consciously think about each of these elements as story elements when they sit down to write, all stories essentially contain these "markers" that make them the stories that they are. But, even though all stories have these elements, they are a lot like fingerprints: Each story's story elements are just a bit different.

Let's look at a few of the most commonly discussed elements. The most commonly discussed story element in fiction is **plot**. Plot is the series of events in a story. Typically, but not always, plot moves in a predictable fashion:

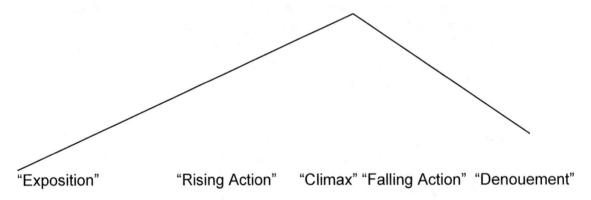

"Exposition"   "Rising Action"   "Climax" "Falling Action" "Denouement"

Exposition is where characters and their situations are introduced. *Rising action* is the point at which conflict starts to occur. *Climax* is the highest point of conflict, often a turning point. *Falling action* is the result of the climax. *Denouement* is the final resolution of the plot.

Character is another commonly studied story element. We will often find in stories heroes, villains, comedic characters, dark characters, etc. When we examine the characters of a story, we look to see who they are and how their traits contribute to the story. Often, because of their characteristics, plot elements become more interesting. For example, authors will pair unlikely characters together somehow that, in turn, creates specific conflict.

The **setting** of a story is the place or location where it occurs. Often, the specific place is not as important as some of the specifics about the setting. For example, the setting of *The Great Gatsby*, New York, is not as significant as the fact that it takes place amongst incredible wealth. Conversely, *The Grapes of Wrath*, although taking place in Oklahoma and California, has a more significant setting of poverty. In fact, as the story takes place *around* other migrant workers, the setting is even more significant. In a way, the setting serves as a reason for various conflicts to occur.

Themes of stories are the underlying messages, above and beyond all plot elements, that writers want to convey. Very rarely will one find that good literature is without a theme—or a lesson, message, or ideal. The best writers in the English language all seem to want to convey something about human nature or the world, and they turn to literature in order to do that. Common themes in literature are jealousy, money, love, human against corporation or government, etc. These themes are never explicitly stated; rather, they are the result of the portrayal of characters, settings, and plots. Readers get the message even if the theme is not directly mentioned.

Finally, the **mood** of a story is the atmosphere or attitude the writer conveys through descriptive language. Often, mood fits in nicely with theme and setting. For example, in Edgar Allen Poe's stories, we often find a mood of horror and darkness. We get that from the descriptions of characters and the setting, as well as from specific plot elements. Mood simply helps us better understand the writer's theme and intentions through descriptive, stylistic language.

COMPETENCY 3.0   UNDERSTAND HOW TO INTERPRET GRAPHIC INFORMATION

Skill 3.1   Interpret information from tables, diagrams, charts, and graphs

Tables

To interpret data in tables, we read across rows and down columns. Each item of interest has different data points listed under different column headings.

Table 1. Sample Purchase Order				
Item	Unit	$/Unit	Qty.	Tot. $
Coffee	lb.	2.79	45	125.55
Milk	gal.	1.05	72	75.60
Sugar	lb.	0.23	150	34.50

In Table 1 (above), the first column on the left contains the items in a purchase order. The other columns contain data about each item labeled with column headings. The second column from the left gives the unit of measurement for each item, the third column gives the price per unit, the fourth column gives the quantity of each item ordered, and the fifth column gives the total cost of each item.

Examples: Use Table 1 to answer the following questions.

1. What does the 1.05 value in the table represent?

   Answer: Price in dollars per gallon of milk.

2. What is the total cost of the purchase order?

   Answer: $235.65

3. How many combined pounds of coffee and sugar does this purchase order purchase?

   Answer: 195 lbs.

Quantitative data is often easily presented in graphs and charts in many content areas. However, if students are unable to decipher the graph, their use becomes limited to students. Since information can clearly be displayed in a graph or chart form, accurate interpretation of the information is an important skill for students.

For graphs, students should be taught to evaluate all the features of the graph, including main title, what the horizontal axis represents and what the vertical axis represents. Also, students should locate and evaluate the graph's key (if there is one) in the event there is more than one variable on the graph. For example, line graphs are often used to plot data from a scientific experiment. If more than one variable was used, a key or legend would indicate what each line on the line graph represented. Then, once students have evaluated the axes and titles, they can begin to assess the results of the experiment.

For charts (such as a pie chart), the process is similar to interpreting bar or line graphs. The key which depicts what each section of the pie chart represents is very important to interpreting the pie chart. Be sure to provide students with lots of assistance and practice with reading and interpreting graphs and charts so their experience with and confidence in reading them develops.

Example: A survey asked five elementary school students to list the number and type of pets they had at home. The first student had three dogs and three fish. The second student had two cats and one dog. The third student had three fish and two dogs. The fourth student had one rabbit, two cats, and one dog. The fifth student had no pets.

Construct a data table and line graph that represents the survey information.

Solution: The following is a table that appropriately represents the data.

Student #	# of Dogs	# of Cats	# of Fish	# of Rabbits	Total # of Pets
1	3	0	3	0	6
2	1	2	0	0	3
3	2	0	3	0	5
4	1	2	0	1	4
5	0	0	0	0	0

The following is a line graph that appropriately represents the total number of pets each student has.

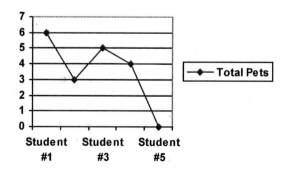

See also Skill 9.1.

Skill 3.2   Recognize appropriate use of graphic formats to represent written information

Sample Passage

Chili peppers may turn out to be the wonder drug of the decade. The fiery fruit comes in many sizes, shapes and colors, all of which grow on plants that are genetic descendants of the tepin plant, originally native to the Americas. Connoisseurs of the regional cuisines of the South west and Louisiana are already well aware that food flavored with chilies can cause a good sweat, but medical researchers are learning more every day about the medical power of capsaicin, the ingredient in the peppers that produces the heat.

Capsaicin as a pain medication has been a part of field medicine for centuries. It is, in fact, the active ingredient in several currently available over-the-counter liniments for sore muscles. Recent research has been examining the value of the compound for the treatment of other painful conditions. Capsaicin shows some promise in the treatment of phantom limb syndrome, as well as shingles, and some types of headaches. Additional research focuses upon the use of capsaicin to relieve pain in post-surgical patients. Scientists speculate that application of the compound to the skin causes the body to release endorphins – natural pain relievers manufactured by the body itself. An alternative theory holds that capsaicin somehow interferes with t transmission of signals along the nerve fibers, thus reducing the sensation of pain.

In addition to its well0documented history as a pain killer, capsaicin has recently received attention as a phytochemical, one of the naturally occurring compounds from foods that show cancer-fighting qualities. Like the phytochemical sulfoaphane found in broccoli, capsaicin might turn out to be an agent capable of short-circuiting the actions of carcinogens at the cell level before they can cause cancer.

Summary: Chili peppers contain a chemical called capsaicin which has proved useful for treating a variety of ailments. Recent research reveals that capsaicin is a phytochemical, a natural compound that may help fight cancer.

Outline: -Chili peppers could be the wonder drug of the decade
-Chili peppers contains capsaicin
-Capsaicin can be used as a pain medication
-Capsaicin is a phytochemical
-Phytochemicals show cancer-fighting qualities
-Capsaicin might be able to short-circuit the effects of carcinogens

Sample Test: Reading

Read the passages and answer the questions that follow.

This writer has often been asked to tutor hospitalized children with cystic fibrosis. While undergoing all the precautionary measures to see these children (i.e. scrubbing thoroughly and donning sterilized protective gear- for the child's protection), she has often wondered why their parents subject these children to the pressures of schooling and trying to catch up on what they have missed because of hospitalization, which is a normal part of cystic fibrosis patients' lives. These children undergo so many tortuous treatments a day that it seems cruel to expect them to learn as normal children do, especially with their life expectancies being as short as they are.

1. **What is meant by the word "precautionary" in the second sentence?**

    A. Careful
    B. Protective
    C. Medical
    D. Sterilizing

2. **What is the author's tone?**

    A. Sympathetic
    B. Cruel
    C. Disbelieving
    D. Cheerful

3. **What is the main idea of this passage?**

    A. There is a lot of preparation involved in visiting a patient of cystic fibrosis.
    B. Children with cystic fibrosis are incapable of living normal lives.
    C. Certain concessions should be made for children with cystic fibrosis.
    D. Children with cystic fibrosis die young.

4. **How is the author so familiar with the procedures used when visiting a child with cystic fibrosis?**

    A. She has read about it.
    B. She works in a hospital.
    C. She is the parent of one.
    D. She often tutors them.

5. **What is the author's purpose?**

    A. To inform
    B. To entertain
    C. To describe
    D. To narrate

6. What type of organizational pattern is the author using?

   A. Classification
   B. Explanation
   C. Comparison and contrast
   D. Cause and effect

7. The author states that it is "cruel" to expect children with cystic fibrosis to learn as "normal" children do. Is this a fact or an opinion?

   A. Fact
   B. Opinion

8. Is there evidence of bias in this paragraph?

   A. Yes
   B. No

9. What kind of relationship is found within the last sentence which starts with "These children undergo..." and ends with "...as short as they are"?

   A. Addition
   B. Explanation
   C. Generalization
   D. Classification

10. Does the author present an argument that is valid or invalid concerning the schooling of children with cystic fibrosis?

    A. Valid
    B. Invalid

Disciplinary practices have been found to affect diverse areas of child development such as the acquisition of moral values, obedience to authority, and performance at school. Even though the dictionary has a specific definition of the word "discipline," it is still open to interpretation by people of different cultures.

There are four types of disciplinary styles: assertion of power, withdrawal of love, reasoning, and permissiveness. Assertion of power involves the use of force to discourage unwanted behavior. Withdrawal of love involves making the love of a parent conditional on a child's good behavior. Reasoning involves persuading the child to behave one way rather than another. Permissiveness involves allowing the child to do as he or she pleases and face the consequences of his/her actions.

11. **What is the meaning of the word "diverse" in the first sentence?**

    A.   Many
    B.   Related to children
    C.   Disciplinary
    D.   Moral

12. **What organizational structure is used in the first sentence of the second paragraph?**

    A.   Addition
    B.   Explanation
    C.   Definition
    D.   Simple listing

13. **Name the four types of disciplinary styles.**

    A.   Reasoning, power assertion, morality, and permissiveness.
    B.   Morality, reasoning, permissiveness, and withdrawal of love.
    C.   Withdrawal of love, permissiveness, assertion of power, and reasoning.
    D.   Permissiveness, morality, reasoning, and power assertion.

14. **What is the main idea of this passage?**

    A.   Different people have different ideas of what discipline is.
    B.   Permissiveness is the most widely used disciplinary style.
    C.   Most people agree on their definition of discipline.
    D.   There are four disciplinary styles.

15. **What is the author's purpose in writing this?**

    A.   To describe
    B.   To narrate
    C.   To entertain
    D.   To inform

16. **Is this passage biased?**

    A.   Yes
    B.   No

17. **What is the author's tone?**

   A. Disbelieving
   B. Angry
   C. Informative
   D. Optimistic

18. **What is the overall organizational pattern of this passage?**

   A. Generalization
   B. Cause and effect
   C. Addition
   D. Summary

19. **The author states that "assertion of power involves the use of force to discourage unwanted behavior." Is this a fact or an opinion?**

   A. Fact
   B. Opinion

20. **From reading this passage we can conclude that**

   A. The author is a teacher.
   B. The author has many children.
   C. The author has written a book about discipline.
   D. The author has done a lot of research on discipline.

21. **What does the technique of reasoning involve?**

   A. Persuading the child to behave in a certain way.
   B. Allowing the child to do as he/she pleases.
   C. Using force to discourage unwanted behavior.
   D. Making love conditional on good behavior.

One of the most difficult problems plaguing American education is the assessment of teachers. No one denies that teachers ought to be answerable for what they do, but what exactly does that mean? The Oxford American Dictionary defines accountability as: the obligation to give a reckoning or explanation for one's actions.

Does a student have to learn for teaching to have taken place? Historically, teaching has not been defined in this restrictive manner; the teacher was thought to be responsible for the quantity and quality of material covered and the way in which it was presented. However, some definitions of teaching now imply that students must learn in order for teaching to have taken place.

As a teacher who tries my best to keep current on all the latest teaching strategies, I believe that those teachers who do not bother even to pick up an educational journal every once in a while should be kept under close watch. There are many teachers out there who have been teaching for decades and refuse to change their ways even if research has proven that their methods are outdated and ineffective. There is no place in the profession of teaching for these types of individuals. It is time that the American educational system clean house, for the sake of our children.

22. **What is the meaning of the word "reckoning" in the third sentence?**

A. Thought
B. Answer
C. Obligation
D. Explanation

23. **What is the organizational pattern of the second paragraph?**

A. Cause and effect
B. Classification
C. Addition
D. Explanation

24. **What is the main idea of the passage?**

A. Teachers should not be answerable for what they do.
B. Teachers who do not do their job should be fired.
C. The author is a good teacher.
D. Assessment of teachers is a serious problem in society today.

25. **Is this a valid argument?**

A. Yes
B. No

Answer Key: Reading

1.	B.	14.	A.
2.	A.	15.	D.
3.	C.	16.	B.
4.	D.	17.	C.
5.	C.	18.	C.
6.	B.	19.	A.
7.	B.	20.	D.
8.	A.	21.	A.
9.	B.	22.	D.
10.	B.	23.	D.
11.	A.	24.	D.
12.	D.	25.	B.
13.	C.		

Rationales for Sample Questions: Reading

1. B. The writer uses expressions such as "protective gear" and "child's protection" to emphasize this.

2. A. The author states that "it seems cruel to expect them to learn as normal children do," thereby indicating that she feels sorry for them.

3. C. The author states that she wonders "why parents subject these children to the pressures of schooling" and that "it seems cruel to expect them to learn as normal children do." In making these statements she appears to be expressing the belief that these children should not have to do what "normal" children do. They have enough to deal with – their illness itself.

4. D. The writer states this fact in the opening sentence.

5. C. The author is simply describing her experience in working with children with cystic fibrosis.

6. B. The author mentions tutoring children with cystic fibrosis in her opening sentence and goes on to "explain" some of these issues that are involved with her job.

7. B. The fact that she states that it "seems" cruel indicates there is no evidence to support this belief.

8. A. The writer clearly feels sorry for these children and gears her writing in that direction.

9. B. In mentioning the their life expectancies are short, she is explaining by giving one reason why it is cruel to expect them to learn as normal children do.

10. B. Even though to most readers, the writer's argument makes good sense, it is biased and lacks real evidence.

11. A. Any of the other choices would be redundant in this sentence.

12. D. The author simply states the types of disciplinary styles.

13. C. This is directly stated in the second paragraph.

14. A. Choice C is not true; the opposite is stated in the passage. Choice B could be true, but we have no evidence of this. Choice D is just one of the many facts listed in the passage.

15. D.   The author is providing the reader with information about disciplinary practices.

16. B.   If the reader were so inclined, he could research discipline and find this information.

17. C.   The author appears to simply be stating the facts.

18. C.   The author has taken a subject, in this case discipline, and developed it point by point.

19. A.   The author appears to have done extensive research on this subject.

20. D.   Given all the facts mentioned in the passage, this is the only inference one can make.

21. A.   This fact is directly stated in the second paragraph.

22. D.   The meaning of this word is directly stated in the same sentence.

23. D.   The author goes on to further explain what she meant by "...what exactly does that mean?" in the first paragraph.

24. D.   Most of the passage is dedicated to elaborating on why teacher assessment is such a problem.

25. B.   In the third paragraph, the author appears to be resentful of lazy teachers.

COMPETENCY 4.0   UNDERSTAND PARTS OF SPEECH, PARTS OF SENTENCES, AND PROPER USAGE IN STANDARD AMERICAN ENGLISH

Skill 4.1   Recognize parts of speech (nouns, pronouns, verbs, adjectives, adverbs, prepositions, conjunctions, interjections)

Plural nouns

The multiplicity and complexity of spelling rules based on phonics, letter doubling, and exceptions to rules - not mastered by adulthood - should be replaced by a good dictionary. As spelling mastery is also difficult for adolescents, our recommendation is the same. Learning the use of a dictionary and thesaurus will be a more rewarding use of time.

Most plurals of nouns that end in hard consonants or hard consonant sounds followed by a silent *e* are made by adding *s*. Some words ending in vowels only add *s*.

fingers, numerals, banks, bugs, riots, homes, gates, radios, bananas

Nouns that end in soft consonant sounds *s, j, x, z, ch,* and *sh,* add *es*. Some nouns ending in *o* add es.

dresses, waxes, churches, brushes, tomatoes

Nouns ending in *y* preceded by a vowel just add *s*.

boys, alleys

Nouns ending in *y* preceded by a consonant change the *y* to *i* and add *es*.

babies, corollaries, frugalities, poppies

Some nouns' plurals are formed irregularly or remain the same.
sheep, deer, children, leaves, oxen

Some nouns derived from foreign words, especially Latin, may make their plurals in two different ways - one of them Anglicized. Sometimes, the meanings are the same; other times, the two plurals are used in slightly different contexts. It is always wise to consult the dictionary.

appendices, appendixes   criterion, criteria
indexes, indices   crisis, crises

Make the plurals of closed (solid) compound words in the usual way except for words ending in *ful* which make their plurals on the root word.

> timelines, hairpins

Make the plurals of open or hyphenated compounds by adding the change in inflection to the word that change in number.

> fathers-in-law, courts-martial, masters of art, doctors of medicine

Make the plurals of letters, numbers, and abbreviations by adding *s*.

> fives and tens, IBMs, 1990s, *p*s and *q*s (Note that letters are italicized.)

Possessive nouns

Make the possessives of singular nouns by adding an apostrophe followed by the letter *s* (*'s*).

> baby's bottle, father's job, elephant's eye, teacher's desk, sympathizer's protests, week's postponement

Make the possessive of singular nouns ending in *s* by adding either an apostrophe or an (*'s*) depending upon common usage or sound. When making the possessive causes difficulty, use a prepositional phrase instead. Even with the sibilant ending, with a few exceptions, it is advisable to use the (*'s*) construction.

> dress's color, species' characteristics or characteristics of the species, James' hat or James's hat, Delores's shirt. Make the possessive of plural nouns ending in *s* by adding the apostrophe after the *s*; horses' coats, jockeys' times, four days' time

Make possessives of plural nouns that do not end in *s* the same as singular nouns by adding *'s*.

> children's shoes, deer's antlers, cattle's horns

Make possessives of compound nouns by adding the inflection at the end of the word or phrase.

> the mayor of Los Angeles' campaign, the mailman's new truck, the mailmen's new trucks, my father-in-law's first wife, the keepsakes' values, several daughters-in-law's husbands

Note: Because a gerund functions as a noun, any noun preceding it and operating as a possessive adjective must reflect the necessary inflection. However, if the gerundive following the noun is a participle, no inflection is added.

> The general was perturbed by the private's sleeping on duty. (The word *sleeping* is a gerund, the object of the preposition *by*.)
> *but*
> The general was perturbed to see the private sleeping on duty. (The word *sleeping* is a participle modifying private.)

Rules for clearly identifying pronoun reference

Make sure that the antecedent reference is clear and cannot refer to something else

A "distant relative" is a relative pronoun or a relative clause that has been placed too far away from the antecedent to which it refers. It is a common error to place a verb between the relative pronoun and its antecedent.

Error: Return the books to the library that are overdue.
Problem: The relative clause "that are overdue" refers to the "books" and should be placed immediately after the antecedent.
Correction: Return the books that are overdue to the library.
> or
> Return the overdue books to the library.

A pronoun should not refer to adjectives or possessive nouns

Adjectives, nouns or possessive pronouns should not be used as antecedents. This will create ambiguity in sentences.

Error: In Todd's letter he told his mom he'd broken the priceless vase.
Problem: In this sentence the pronoun "he" seems to refer to the noun phrase "Todd's letter" though it was probably meant to refer to the possessive noun "Todd's."
Correction: In his letter, Todd told his mom that he had broken the priceless vase.

A pronoun should not refer to an implied idea

A pronoun must refer to a specific antecedent rather than an implied antecedent. When an antecedent is not stated specifically, the reader has to guess or assume the meaning of a sentence. Pronouns that do not have antecedents are called expletives. "It" and "there" are the most common expletives, though other pronouns can also become expletives as well. In informal conversation, expletives allow for casual presentation of ideas without supporting evidence. However, in more formal writing, it is best to be more precise.

Error: She said that it is important to floss every day.
Problem: The pronoun "it" refers to an implied idea.
Correction: She said that flossing every day is important.

Error: They returned the book because there were missing pages.
Problem: The pronouns "they" and "there" do not refer to the antecedent.
Correction: The customer returned the book with missing pages.

Using Who, That and Which

Who, whom and **whose** refer to human beings and can either introduce essential or nonessential clauses. **That** refers to things other than humans and is used to introduce essential clauses. **Which** refers to things other than humans and is used to introduce nonessential clauses.

Error: The doctor that performed the surgery said the man would be fully recovered.
Problem: Since the relative pronoun is referring to a human, who should be used.
Correction: The doctor who performed the surgery said the man would be fully recovered.

Error: That ice cream cone that you just ate looked really delicious.
Problem: That has already been used so you must use *which* to introduce the next clause, whether it is essential or nonessential.
Correction: That ice cream cone, which you just ate, looked really delicious.

Proper case forms

Pronouns, unlike nouns, change case forms. Pronouns must be in the subjective, objective, or possessive form according to their function in the sentence.

|---|---|---|---|---|---|
	Subjective (Nominative)		Possessive		Objective	
	Singular	Plural	Singular	Plural	Singular	Plural
1st person	I	We	My	Our	Me	Us
2nd person	You	You	Your	Your	You	You
3rd person	He She It	They	His Her Its	Their	Him Her It	them

Relative Pronouns

Who   Subjective/Nominative
Whom   Objective
Whose   Possessive

Error: Tom and me have reserved seats for next week's baseball game.

Problem: The pronoun *me* is the subject of the verb *have reserved* and should be in the subjective form.

Correction: *Tom and I have reserved seats for next week's baseball game.*

Error: Who's coat is this?

Problem: The interrogative possessive pronoun is whose; *who's* is the contraction for who is.

Correction: *Whose coat is this?*

Error: The voters will choose the candidate whom has the best qualifications for the job.

Problem: The case of the relative pronoun who or whom is determined by the pronoun's function in the clause in which it appears. The word who is in the subjective case, and whom is in the objective. Analyze how the pronoun is being used within the sentence.

Correction: *The voters will choose the candidate who has the best qualifications for the job.*

PRACTICE EXERCISE – PRONOUN CASE

Choose the option that corrects an error in the underlined portion(s).
If no error exists, choose "No change is necessary".

1)   Even though Sheila and <u>he</u> had planned to be alone at the diner, <u>they</u> were joined by three friends of <u>their's</u> instead.

     A) him
     B) him and her
     ✓C) theirs
     D) No change is necessary.

2)   Uncle Walter promised to give his car to <u>whomever</u> will guarantee to drive it safely.

     A) whom
     ✓B) whoever
     C) them
     D) No change is necessary.

3)   Eddie and <u>him</u> gently laid <u>the body</u> on the ground next to <u>the sign</u>.

     ✓A) he
     B) them
     C) it
     D) No change is necessary.

4)   Mary, <u>who</u> is competing in the chess tournament, is a better player than <u>me</u>.

     A) whose
     B) whom
     ✓C) I
     D) No change is necessary.

5)   <u>We, ourselves,</u> have decided not to buy property in that development; however, our friends have already bought <u>themselves</u> some land.

     A) We, ourself,
     B) their selves
     C) their self
     D) No change is necessary.

ANSWER KEY : PRACTICE EXERCISE FOR PRONOUN CASE

1) C   The possessive pronoun *theirs* doesn't need an apostrophe.
Option A is incorrect because the subjective pronoun *he* is
needed in this sentence. Option B is incorrect because the
subjective pronoun *they*, not the objective pronouns *him*
and *her*, is needed.

2) B   The subjective case *whoever*--not the objective case *whomever*
--is the subject of the relative clause *whoever will guarantee to
drive it safely*. Option A is incorrect because *whom* is an
objective pronoun. Option C is incorrect because *car* is singular
and takes the pronoun *it*.

3) A   The subjective pronoun *he* is needed as the subject of the verb
laid. Option B is incorrect because *them* is vague; the noun *body*
is needed to clarify *it*. Option C is incorrect because *it* is vague,
and the noun *sign* is necessary for clarification.

4) C   The subjective pronoun *I* is needed because the comparison is
understood. Option A incorrectly uses the possessive *whose*.
Option B is incorrect because the subjective pronoun *who*, and
not the objective *whom*, is needed.

5) B   The reflexive pronoun *themselves* refers to the plural *friends*.
Option A is incorrect because the plural *we* requires the
reflexive *ourselves*. Option C is incorrect because the
possessive pronoun *their* is never joined with either *self* or
selves.

Past tense and past participles

Both regular and irregular verbs must appear in their standard forms for each tense. Note: the ed or d ending is added to regular verbs in the past tense and for past participles.

Infinitive	Past Tense	Past Participle
Bake	Baked	Baked

Irregular Verb Forms

Infinitive	Past Tense	Past Participle
Be	Was, were	Been
Become	Became	Become
Break	Broke	Broken
Bring	Brought	Brought
Choose	Chose	Chosen
Come	Came	Come
Do	Did	Done
Draw	Drew	Drawn
Eat	Ate	Eaten
Fall	Fell	Fallen
Forget	Forgot	Forgotten
Freeze	Froze	Frozen
Give	Gave	Given
Go	Went	Gone
Grow	Grew	Grown
Have/has	Had	Had
Hide	Hid	Hidden
Know	Knew	Known
Lay	Laid	Laid
Lie	Lay	Lain
Ride	Rode	Ridden
Rise	Rose	Risen
Run	Ran	Run
See	Saw	Seen
Steal	Stole	Stolen
Take	Took	Taken
Tell	Told	Told
Throw	Threw	Thrown
Wear	Wore	Worn
Write	Wrote	Written

Error: She should have went to her doctor's appointment at the scheduled time.

Problem: The past participle of the verb *to go* is *gone*. *Went* expresses the simple past tense.

Correction: *She should have gone to her doctor's appointment at the scheduled time.*

Error: My train is suppose to arrive before two o'clock.

Problem: The verb following *train* is a present tense passive construction which requires the present tense verb *to be* and the past participle.

Correction: *My train is supposed to arrive before two o'clock.*

Error: Linda should of known that the car wouldn't start after leaving it out in the cold all night.

Problem: *Should of* is a nonstandard expression. *Of is* not a verb.

Correction: *Linda should have known that the car wouldn't start after leaving it out in the cold all night.*

PRACTICE EXERCISE – STANDARD VERB FORMS

Choose the option that corrects an error in the underlined portion(s). If no error exists, choose "No change is necessary."

1)   My professor _had knew_ all along that we would pass his course.

   A. know
   B. had known
   C. knowing
   D. No change is necessary.

2)   Kevin was asked to erase the vulgar words he _had wrote._

   A. writes
   B. has write
   C. had written
   D. No change is necessary.

3)   Melanie _had forget_ to tell her parents that she left the cat in the closet.

   A. had forgotten
   B. forgot
   C. forget
   D. No change is necessary.

4)   Craig always _leave_ the house a mess when his parents aren't there.

   A. left
   B. leaves
   C. leaving
   D. No change is necessary.

5)   The store manager accused Kathy of _having stole_ more than five hundred dollars from the safe.

   A. has stolen
   B. having stolen
   C. stole
   D. No change is necessary.

ANSWER KEY : PRACTICE EXERCISE FOR STANDARD VERB FORMS

1. B   Option B is correct because the past participle needs the helping verb *had*. Option A is incorrect because *it* is in the infinitive tense. Option C incorrectly uses the present participle.

2. C   Option C is correct because the past participle follows the helping verb *had*. Option A uses the verb in the present tense. Option B is an incorrect use of the verb.

3. A   Option A is correct because the past participle uses the helping verb *had*. Option B uses the wrong form of the verb. Option C uses the wrong form of the verb.

4. B   Option B correctly uses the past tense of the verb. Option A uses the verb in an incorrect way. Option C uses the verb without a helping verb like *is*.

5. B   Option B is correct because it is the past participle. Option A and C use the verb incorrectly.

Correct use of adjectives and adverbs

Adjectives are words that modify or describe nouns or pronouns. Adjectives usually precede the words they modify, but not always; for example, an adjective occurs after a linking verb.

Adverbs are words that modify verbs, adjectives, or other adverbs. They cannot modify nouns. Adverbs answer such questions as how, why, when, where, how much, or how often something is done. Many adverbs are formed by adding ly.

Error: The birthday cake tasted sweetly.

Problem: *Tasted* is a linking verb; the modifier that follows should be an adjective, not an adverb.

Correction: *The birthday cake tasted sweet.*

Error: You have done good with this project.

Problem: *Good* is an adjective and cannot be used to modify a verb phrase such as have done.

Correction: *You have done well with this project.*

Error: The coach was positive happy about the team's chance of winning.

Problem: The adjective *positive* cannot be used to modify another adjective, *happy*. An adverb is needed instead.

Correction: *The coach was positively happy about the team's chance of winning.*

Error: The fireman acted quick and brave to save the child from the burning building.

Problem: *Quick and brave* are adjectives and cannot be used to describe a verb. Adverbs are needed instead.

Correction: *The fireman acted quickly and bravely to save the child from the burning building.*

PRACTICE EXERCISE – ADJECTIVES AND ADVERBS

Choose the option that corrects an error in the underlined portion(s).
If no error exists, choose "No change is necessary."

1)   Moving quick throughout the house, the burglar removed several
        priceless antiques before carelessly dropping his wallet.

        ✓A) quickly
         B) remove
         C) careless
         D) No change is necessary.

2)   The car crashed loudly into the retaining wall before spinning wildly
        on the sidewalk.

         A) crashes
         B) loudly
         C) wild
        ✓D) No change is necessary.

3)   The airplane landed safe on the runway after nearly colliding with
        a helicopter.

         A) land
        ✓B) safely
         C) near
         D) No change is necessary.

4)   The horribly bad special effects in the movie disappointed us great.

         A) horrible
         B) badly
        ✓C) greatly
         D) No change is necessary.

5)   The man promised to faithfully obey the rules of the social club.

         A) faithful
         B) faithfulness
         C) faith
        ✓D) No change is necessary.

ANSWER KEY: PRACTICE EXERCISE FOR ADJECTIVES AND ADVERBS

1) A   The adverb *quickly* is needed to modify *moving*. Option B is incorrect because it uses the wrong form of the verb. Option C is incorrect because the adverb *carelessly* is needed before the verb *dropping,* not the adjective *careless*.

2) D   The sentence is correct as it is written. Adverbs *loudly* and *wildly* are needed to modify *crashed* and *spinning*. Option A incorrectly uses the verb *crashes* instead of the participle *crashing*, which acts as an adjective.

3) B   The adverb *safely* is needed to modify the verb *landed*. Option A is incorrect because *land* is a noun. Option C is incorrect because *near* is an adjective, not an adverb.

4) C   The adverb *greatly* is needed to modify the verb *disappointed*. Option A is incorrect because *horrible* is an adjective, not an adverb. Option B is incorrect because *bad* needs to modify the adverb *horribly*.

5) D   The adverb *faithfully* is the correct modifier of the verb *promised*. Option A is an adjective used to modify nouns. Neither Option B nor Option C, which are both nouns, is a modifier.

Skill 4.2   Recognize parts of a sentence (e.g., subject, verb, complement)

Sentence structure

Recognize simple, compound, complex, and compound-complex sentences. Use dependent (subordinate) and independent clauses correctly to create these sentence structures.

Simple – Consists of one independent clause
> Joyce wrote a letter.

Compound – Consists of two or more independent clauses. The two clauses are usually connected by a coordinating conjunction (and, but, or, nor, for, so, yet). Compound sentences are sometimes connected by semicolons.
> Joyce wrote a letter, and Dot drew a picture.

Complex- Consists of an independent clause plus one or more dependent clauses. The dependent clause may precede the independent clause or follow it.
> While Joyce wrote a letter, Dot drew a picture.

Compound/Complex – Consists of one or more dependent clauses plus two or more independent clauses .
> When Mother asked the girls to demonstrate their new-found skills, Joyce wrote a letter, and Dot drew a picture.

Note: Do **not** confuse compound sentence elements with compound sentences.

> Simple sentence with compound subject
>> <u>Joyce</u> and <u>Dot</u> wrote letters.
>> The <u>girl</u> in row three and the <u>boy</u> next to her were passing notes across the aisle.

> Simple sentence with compound predicate
>> Joyce <u>wrote letters</u> and <u>drew pictures</u>.
>> The captain of the high school debate team <u>graduated with honors</u> and <u>studied broadcast journalism in college</u>.

> Simple sentence with compound object of preposition
>> Coleen graded the students' essays for <u>style</u> and <u>mechanical accuracy</u>.

Types of Clauses

Clauses are connected word groups that are composed of *at least* one subject and one verb. (A subject is the doer of an action or the element that is being joined. A verb conveys either the action or the link.)

Students are waiting for the start of the assembly.
Subject   Verb

At the end of the play, students wait for the curtain to come down.
                              Subject   Verb

Clauses can be independent or dependent.

Independent clauses can stand alone or can be joined to other clauses.

Independent clause	for and nor	
Independent clause,	but or yet so	Independent clause
Independent clause	;	Independent clause
Dependent clause	,	Independent clause
Independent clause		Dependent clause

Dependent clauses, by definition, contain at least one subject and one verb. However, they cannot stand alone as a complete sentence. They are structurally dependent on the main clause.

There are two types of dependent clauses: (1) those with a subordinating conjunction, and (2) those with a relative pronoun

Sample coordinating conjunctions:
Although
When
If
Unless
Because

Unless a cure is discovered, many more people will die of the disease.
    Dependent clause   +   Independent clause

Sample relative pronouns:
Who
Whom
Which
That

The White House has an official website, which contains press releases, news updates, and biographies of the President and Vice-President.
(Independent clause + relative pronoun + relative dependent clause)

Skill 4.3   **Recognize the standard use of verbs (e.g., subject-verb agreement, verb tense)**

Verb tenses must refer to the same time period consistently, unless a change in time is required.

Error: Despite the increased amount of students in the school this year, overall attendance is higher last year at the sporting events.

Problem: The verb *is* represents an inconsistent shift to the present tense when the action refers to a past occurrence.

Correction: *Despite the increased amount of students in the school this year, overall attendance was higher last year at sporting events.*

Error: My friend Lou, who just competed in the marathon, ran since he was twelve years old.

Problem: Because Lou continues to run, the present perfect tense is needed.

Correction: *My friend Lou, who just competed in the marathon, has ran since he was twelve years old.*

Error: The Mayor congratulated Wallace Mangham, who renovates the city hall last year.

Problem: Although the speaker is talking in the present, the action of renovating the city hall was in the past.

Correction: *The Mayor congratulated Wallace Mangham, who renovated the city hall last year.*

PRACTICE EXERCISE – SHIFTS IN TENSE

Choose the option that corrects an error in the underlined portion(s).
If no error exists, choose "No change is necessary".

1)   After we <u>washed</u> the fruit that had <u>growing</u> in the garden, we knew
      there <u>was</u> a store that would buy them.

      A) washing
      B) grown
      C) is
      D) No change is necessary.

2)   The tourists <u>used</u> to visit the Atlantic City boardwalk whenever they
      <u>vacationed</u> during the summer. Unfortunately, their numbers have
      <u>diminished</u> every year.

      A) use
      B) vacation
      C) diminish
      D) No change is necessary.

3)   When the temperature <u>drops</u> to below thirty-two degrees Fahrenheit,
      the water on the lake <u>freezes</u>, which <u>allowed</u> children to skate across it.

      A) dropped
      B) froze
      C) allows
      D) No change is necessary.

4)   The artists were <u>hired</u> to <u>create</u> a monument that would pay tribute to
      the men who were <u>killed</u> in World War Two.

      A) hiring
      B) created
      C) killing
      D) No change is necessary.

5)   Emergency medical personnel rushed to the scene of the shooting,
      where many injured people <u>waiting</u> for treatment.

      A) wait
      B) waited
      C) waits
      D) No change is necessary.

ANSWER KEY : PRACTICE EXERCISE FOR SHIFTS IN TENSE

1) B   The past participle *grown* is needed instead of *growing* which is the progressive tense. Option A is incorrect because the past participle *washed* takes the *ed*. Option C incorrectly replaces the past participle *was* with the present tense *is*.

2) D   Option A is incorrect because *use* is the present tense. Option B incorrectly uses the noun *vacation*. Option C incorrectly uses the present tense *diminish* instead of the past tense *diminished*.

3) C   The present tense *allows* is necessary in the context of the sentence. Option A is incorrect because *dropped* is a past participle. Option B is incorrect because *froze* is also a past participle.

4) D   In Option A is incorrect because *hiring* is the present tense. In Option B is incorrect because *created* is a past participle. In Option C, *killing*, doesn't fit into the context of the sentence.

5) B   In Option B, *waited*, corresponds with the past tense *rushed*. In Option A, *wait*, is incorrect because it is present tense. In Option C, *waits*, is incorrect because the noun *people* is plural and requires the singular form of the verb.

Agreement between subject and verb

A verb must correspond in the singular or plural form with the simple subject; it is not affected by any interfering elements. Note: A simple subject is never found in a prepositional phrase (a phrase beginning with a word such as of, by, over, through, until).

Present Tense Verb Form

	Singular	Plural
1st person (talking about oneself)	I do	We do
2nd person (talking to another)	You do	You do
3rd person (talking about someone or something)	He She does It	They do

Error: Sally, as well as her sister, plan to go into nursing.

Problem: The subject in the sentence is *Sally* alone, not the word *sister*. Therefore, the verb must be singular.

Correction: *Sally, as well as her sister, plans to go into nursing.*

Error: There has been many car accidents lately on that street.

Problem: The subject accidents in this sentence is plural; the verb must be plural also --even though it comes before the subject.

Correction: *There have been many car accidents lately on that street.*

Error: Everyone of us have a reason to attend the school musical.

Problem: The simple subject is the word *everyone*, not the *us* in the prepositional phrase. Therefore, the verb must be singular also.

Correction: *Everyone of us has a reason to attend the school musical.*

Error: Either the police captain or his officers is going to the convention.

Problem: In either/or and neither/nor constructions, the verb agrees with the subject closer to it.

Correction: *Either the police captain or his officers are going to the convention.*

PRACTICE EXERCISE – SUBJECT-VERB AGREEMENT

Choose the option that corrects an error in the underlined portion(s).
If no error exists, choose "No change is necessary."

1) Every year ,the store <u>stays</u> open late, when shoppers desperately <u>try</u> to purchase Christmas presents as they <u>prepare</u> for the holiday.

    A. stay
    B. tries
    C. prepared
    D. No change is necessary.

2) Paul McCartney, together with George Harrison and Ringo Starr, <u>sing</u> classic Beatles songs on a special greatest-hits CD.

    A. singing
    B. sings
    C. sung
    D. No change is necessary.

3) My friend's cocker spaniel, while <u>chasing</u> cats across the street, always <u>manages</u> to <u>knock</u> over the trash cans.

    A. chased
    B. manage
    C. knocks
    D. No change is necessary.

4) Some of the ice on the driveway <u>have melted.</u>

    A. having melted
    B. has melted
    C. has melt.
    D. No change is necessary.

5) Neither the criminal forensics expert nor the DNA blood evidence <u>provided</u> enough support for that verdict.

    A. provides
    B. were providing
    C. are providing
    D. No change is necessary.

ANSWER KEY: PRACTICE EXERCISE FOR SUBJECT-VERB AGREEMENT

1) D Option D is correct because *store* is third person singular and requires the third person singular verbs *stays*. Option B is incorrect because the plural noun *shoppers* requires a plural verb *try*. In Option C, there is no reason to shift to the past tense *prepared*.

2) B Option B is correct because the subject, *Paul McCartney,* is singular and requires the singular verb *sings*. Option A is incorrect because the present participle *singing* does not stand alone as a verb. Option C is incorrect because the past participle *sung* alone cannot function as the verb in this sentence.

3) D Option D is the correct answer because the subject *cocker spaniel* is singular and requires the singular verb *manages*. Options A,B, and C do not work structurally with the sentence.

4) B The subject of the sentence is *some*, which requires a third person singular verb, *has melted*. Option A incorrectly uses the present participle *having*, which does not act as a helping verb. Option C does not work structurally with the sentence.

5) A In Option A, the singular subject *evidence* is closer to the verb and thus requires the singular in the neither/nor construction. Both Options B and C are plural forms with the helping verb and the present participle.

Skill 4.4   Recognize the standard use of pronouns (e.g., pronoun-antecedent agreement)

Agreements between pronoun and antecedent

A pronoun must correspond to its antecedent in number (singular or plural), person (first, second or third person) and gender (male, female or neutral). A pronoun must refer clearly to a single word, not to a complete idea.

A **pronoun shift** is a grammatical error in which the author starts a sentence, paragraph, or section of a paper using one particular type of pronoun and then suddenly shifts to another. This often confuses the reader.

Error: A teacher should treat all their students fairly.

Problem: Since *A teacher* is singular, the pronoun referring to it must also be singular. Otherwise, the noun has to be made plural.

Correction: *Teachers should treat all their students fairly.*

Error: When an actor is rehearsing for a play, it often helps if you can memorize the lines in advance.

Problem: *Actor* is a third-person word; that is, the writer is talking about the subject. The pronoun *you* is in the second person, which means the writer is talking to the subject.

Correction: *When actors are rehearsing for plays, it helps if they can memorize the lines in advance.*

Error: The workers in the factory were upset when his or her paychecks didn't arrive on time.

Problem: *Workers* is a plural form, while *his or her* refers to one person.

Correction: *The workers in the factory were upset when their paychecks didn't arrive on time.*

Error: The charity auction was highly successful, which pleased everyone.

Problem: In this sentence the pronoun *which* refers to the idea of the auction's success. In fact, *which* has no antecedent in the sentence; the word success is not stated.

Correction: *Everyone was pleased at the success of the auction.*

Error: Lana told Melanie that she would like aerobics.
Problem: The person that she refers to is unclear; it could be either Lana or Melanie.

Correction: *Lana said that Melanie would like aerobics.*

OR

Lana told Melanie that she, Melanie, would like aerobics.

Error: I dislike accounting, even though my brother is one.

Problem: A person's occupation is not the same as a field, and the pronoun *one* is thus incorrect. Note that the word *accountant* is not used in the sentence, so *one* has no antecedent.

Correction: *I dislike accounting, even though my brother is an accountant.*

PRACTICE EXERCISE – PRONOUN/ANTECEDENT AGREEMENT

Choose the option that corrects an error in the underlined portion(s).
If no error exists, choose "No change is necessary."

1)   You can get to Martha's Vineyard by driving from Boston to Woods
      Hole. Once there, you can travel over on a ship, but you may find
      traveling by airplane to be an exciting experience.
      A. they
      B. visitors
      C. it
      D. No change is necessary.

2)   Both the city leader and the journalist are worried about the new
      interstate; she fears the new roadway will destroy precious farmland.
      A. journalist herself
      B. they fear
      C. it
      D. No change is necessary.

3)   When hunters are looking for deer in the woods, you must remain
      quiet for long periods of time.
      A. they
      B. it
      C. we
      D. No change is necessary.

4)   Florida's strong economy is based on the importance of the citrus
      industry. Producing orange juice for most of the country.
      A. They produce
      B. Who produce
      C. Farmers there produce
      D. No change is necessary.

5)   Dr. Kennedy told Paul Elliot, his assistant, that he would have to
      finish grading the tests before going home, no matter how long it
      took.
      A. their
      B. he, Paul
      C. they
      D. No change is necessary.

ANSWER KEY: PRACTICE EXERCISE FOR PRONOUN AGREEMENT

1) D — Pronouns must be consistent. As *you* is used throughout the sentence, the shift to *visitors* is incorrect. Option A, *They*, is vague and unclear. Option C, *it*, is also unclear.

2) B — The plural pronoun *they* is necessary to agree with the two nouns *leader* and *journalist*. There is no need for the reflexive pronoun *herself* in Option A. Option C, *it*, is vague.

3) A — The shift to *you* is unnecessary. The plural pronoun *they* is necessary to agree with the noun *hunters*. The word *we* in Option C is vague; the reader does not know who the word *we* might refer to. Option B, *it*, has no antecedent.

4) C — The noun *farmers* is needed for clarification because *producing* is vague. Option A is incorrect because *they produce* is vague. Option B is incorrect because *who* has no antecedent and creates a fragment.

5) B — The repetition of the name *Paul* is necessary to clarify who the pronoun *he* is referring to. (It could be Dr. Kennedy.) Option A is incorrect because the singular pronoun *his* is needed, not the plural pronoun *their*. Option C is incorrect because the pronoun *it* refers to the plural noun *tests*.

Skill 4.5   Recognize the standard use of modifiers (e.g., adjectives, adverbs)

Particular phrases that are not placed near the one word they modify often result in misplaced **modifiers**. Particular phrases that do not relate to the subject being modified result in dangling modifiers.

Error: Weighing the options carefully, a decision was made regarding the punishment of the convicted murderer.

Problem: Who is weighing the options? No one capable of weighing is named in the sentence; thus, the participle phrase *weighing the options carefully* dangles. This problem can be corrected by adding a subject of the sentence capable of doing the action.

Correction: *Weighing the options carefully, the judge made a decision regarding the punishment of the convicted murderer.*

Error: Returning to my favorite watering hole, brought back many fond memories.

Problem: The person who returned is never indicated, and the participle phrase dangles. This problem can be corrected by creating a dependent clause from the modifying phrase.

Correction: *When I returned to my favorite watering hole, many fond memories came back to me.*

Error: Recovered from the five-mile hike, the obstacle course was a piece of cake for the Boy Scout troop.

Problem: The obstacle course is not recovered from the five-mile hike, so the modifying phrase must be placed closer to the word, *troop*, that it modifies.

Correction: *The obstacle course was a piece of cake for the Boy Scout troop, which had just recovered from a five-mile hike.*

PRACTICE EXERCISE – MISPLACED AND DANGLING MODIFIERS

Choose the sentence that expresses the thought most clearly and effectively and that has no error in structure.

1)   A. Attempting to remove the dog from the well, the paramedic tripped and fell in also.

       B. As the paramedic attempted to remove the dog from the well, he tripped and fell in also.

       C. The paramedic tripped and fell in also attempting to remove the dog from the well.

2)   A. To save the wounded child, a powerful explosion ripped through the operating room as the doctors worked.

       B. In the operating room, as the wounded child was being saved, a powerful explosion ripped through.

       C. To save the wounded child, the doctors worked as an explosion ripped through the operating room.

3)   A. One hot July morning, a herd of giraffes screamed wildly in the jungle next to the wildlife habitat.

       B. One hot July morning, a herd of giraffes screamed in the jungle wildly next to the wildlife habitat.

       C. One hot July morning, a herd of giraffes screamed in the jungle next to the wildlife habitat, wildly.

4)   A. Looking through the file cabinets in the office, the photographs of the crime scene revealed a new suspect in the investigation.

       B. Looking through the file cabinets in the office, the detective discovered photographs of the crime scene which revealed a new suspect in the investigation.

       C. A new suspect in the investigation was revealed in photographs of the crime scene that were discovered while looking through the file cabinets in the office.

ANSWER KEY: PRACTICE EXERCISE FOR MISPLACED AND DANGLING MODIFIERS

1) B   Option B corrects the dangling participle *attempting to remove the dog from the well* by creating a dependent clause introducing the main clause. In Option A, the introductory participle phrase *Attempting...well* does not refer to a paramedic, the subject of the main clause. The word also in Option C incorrectly implies that the paramedic was doing something besides trying to remove the dog.

2) C   Option C corrects the dangling modifier *to save the wounded child* by adding the concrete subject doctors worked. Option A infers that an explosion was working to save the wounded child. Option B never tells who was trying to save the wounded child.

3) A   Option A places the adverb *wildly* closest to the verb screamed, which it modifies. Both Options B and C incorrectly place the modifier away from the verb.

4) B   Option B corrects the modifier *looking through the file cabinets in the office* by placing it next to the detective who is doing the looking. Option A sounds as though the photographs were looking; Option C has no one doing the looking.

Appropriate comparative and superlative degree forms

When comparisons are made, the correct form of the adjective or adverb must be used. The comparative form is used for two items. The superlative form is used for more than two.

	Comparative	Superlative
slow	slower	slowest
young	younger	youngest
tall	taller	tallest

With some words, more and most are used to make comparisons instead of er and est.

quiet	more quiet	most quiet
energetic	more energetic	most energetic
quick	more quickly	most quickly

Comparisons must be made between similar structures or items. In the sentence, "My house is similar in color to Steve's," one house is being compared to another house as understood by the use of the possessive Steve's.

On the other hand, if the sentence reads "My house is similar in color to Steve," the comparison would be faulty because it would be comparing the house to Steve, not to Steve's house.

Error: Last year's rides at the carnival were bigger than this year.

Problem: In the sentence as it is worded above, the rides at the carnival are being compared to this year, not to this year's rides.

Correction: *Last year's rides at the carnival were bigger than this year's.*

PRACTICE EXERCISE – LOGICAL COMPARISONS

Choose the sentence that logically and correctly expresses the comparison.

1) A. This year's standards are higher than last year.
    B. This year's standards are more high than last year.
    C. This year's standards are higher than last year's.

2) A. Tom's attitudes are very different from his father's.
    B. Toms attitudes are very different from his father.
    C. Tom's attitudes are very different from his father.

3) A. John is the stronger member of the gymnastics team.
    B. John is the strongest member of the gymnastics team.
    C. John is the most strong member of the gymnastics team.

4) A. Tracy's book report was longer than Tony's.
    B. Tracy's book report was more long than Tony's.
    C. Tracy's book report was longer than Tony.

5) A. Becoming a lawyer is as difficult as, if not more difficult than, becoming a doctor.

    B. Becoming a lawyer is as difficult, if not more difficult than, becoming a doctor.

    C. Becoming a lawyer is difficult, if not more difficult than, becoming a doctor.

6) A. Better than any movie of the modern era, *Schindler's List* portrays the destructiveness of hate.

    B. More better than any movie of the modern era, *Schindler's List* portrays the destructiveness of hate.

    C. Better than any other movie of the modern era, *Schindler's List* portrays the destructiveness of hate.

ANSWER KEY: PRACTICE EXERCISE FOR LOGICAL COMPARISONS

1) C   Option C is correct because the comparison is between this year's standards and last year's [standards is understood]. Option A compares the standards to last year. In Option B, the faulty comparative *more high* should be higher.

2) A   Option A is incorrect because Tom's attitudes are compared to his father's [attitudes is understood]. Option B deletes the necessary apostrophe to show possession (Tom's), and the comparison is faulty with *attitudes* compared to father. While Option C uses the correct possessive, it retains the faulty comparison shown in Option B.

3) B   In Option B, John is correctly the strongest member of a team that consists of more than two people. Option A uses the comparative *stronger* (comparison of two items) rather than the superlative *stronges*t (comparison of more than two). Option C uses a faulty superlative most strong.

4) A   Option A is correct because the comparison is between Tracy's book report and Tony's (book report). Option B uses the faulty comparative *more long* instead of longer. Option C wrongly compares Tracy's book report to Tony.

5) A   In Option A, the dual comparison is correctly stated: *as difficult as, if not more difficult than*. Remember to test the dual comparison by taking out the intervening comparison. Option B deletes the necessary *as* after the first *difficult*. Option C deletes the *as* before and after the first *difficult*.

6) C   Option C includes the necessary word *other* in the comparison *better than any other movie*. The comparison in Option A is not complete, and Option B uses a faulty comparative *more better*.

COMPETENCY 5.0   UNDERSTAND AND APPLY BASIC PRINCIPLES OF GOOD WRITING

Skill 5.1   Recognize the use of writing for different audiences and purposes (e.g., business letter, newspaper article, advertisement)

An essay is an extended discussion of a writer's point of view about a particular topic. This point of view may be supported by using such writing modes as examples, argument and persuasion, analysis or comparison/contrast. In any case, a good essay is clear, coherent, well-organized and fully developed.

When an author sets out to write a passage, he/she usually has a purpose for doing so. That purpose may be to simply give information that might be interesting or useful to some reader or other; it may be to persuade the reader to a point of view or to move the reader to act in a particular way; it may be to tell a story; or it may be to describe something in such a way that an experience becomes available to the reader through one of the five senses. Following are the primary devices for expressing a particular purpose in a piece of writing:

- **Basic expository writing** simply gives information not previously known about a topic or is used to explain or define one. Facts, examples, statistics, cause and effect, direct tone, objective rather than subjective delivery, and non-emotional information is presented in a formal manner.
- **Descriptive writing** centers on person, place, or object, using concrete and sensory words to create a mood or impression and arranging details in a chronological or spatial sequence.
- **Narrative writing** is developed using an incident or anecdote or related series of events. Chronology, the 5 W's, topic sentence, and conclusion are essential ingredients.
- **Persuasive writing** implies the writer's ability to select vocabulary and arrange facts and opinions in such a way as to direct the actions of the listener/reader. Persuasive writing may incorporate exposition and narration as they illustrate the main idea.
- **Journalistic writing** is theoretically free of author bias. It is essential when relaying information about an event, person, or thing that it be factual and objective. Provide students with an opportunity to examine newspapers and create their own. Many newspapers have educational programs that are offered free to schools.

Tailoring language for a particular **audience** is an important skill. Writing to be read by a business associate will surely sound different from writing to be read by a younger sibling. Not only are the vocabularies different, but the formality/informality of the discourse will need to be adjusted.

The things to be aware of in determining what the language should be for a particular audience, then, hinges on two things: **word choice** and formality/informality. The most formal language does not use contractions or slang. The most informal language will probably feature a more casual use of common sayings and anecdotes. Formal language will use longer sentences and will not sound like a conversation. The most informal language will use shorter sentences—not necessarily simple sentences—but shorter constructions and may sound like a conversation.

In both formal and informal writing there exists a **tone**, the writer's attitude toward the material and/or readers. Tone may be playful, formal, intimate, angry, serious, ironic, outraged, baffled, tender, serene, depressed, etc. The overall tone of a piece of writing is dictated by both the subject matter and the audience. Tone is also related to the actual words which make up the document, as we attach affective meanings to words, called **connotations**. Gaining this conscious control over language makes it possible to use language appropriately in various situations and to evaluate its uses in literature and other forms of communication. By evoking the proper responses from readers/listeners, we can prompt them to take action.

The following questions are an excellent way to assess the audience and tone of a given piece of writing.

1. Who is your audience? (friend, teacher, business person, someone else)
2. How much does this person know about you and/or your topic?
3. What is your purpose? (to prove an argument, to persuade, to amuse, to register a complaint, to ask for a raise)
4. What emotions do you have about the topic? (nervous, happy, confident, angry, sad, no feelings at all)
5. What emotions do you want to register with your audience? (anger, nervousness, happiness, boredom, interest)
6. What persona do you need to create in order to achieve your purpose?
7. What choice of language is best suited to achieving your purpose with your particular subject? (slang, friendly but respectful, formal)
8. What emotional quality do you want to transmit to achieve your purpose (matter of fact, informative, authoritative, inquisitive, sympathetic, angry) and to what degree do you want to express this tone?

Skill 5.2   Identify effective topic sentences and supporting details

Topic Sentences

Just as the essay must have an overall focus reflected in the thesis statement, each paragraph must have a central idea reflected in the topic sentence. A good topic sentence also provides transition from the previous paragraph and relates to the essay's thesis. Good topic sentences, therefore, provide unity throughout the essay.

Consider the following potential topic sentences. Be sure that each provides transition and clearly states the subject of the paragraph.

Topic Sentence 1: *Computers are used in science.*

Analysis: This sentence simply states the topic--computers used in science. It does not relate to the thesis or provide transition from the introduction. The reader still does not know how computers are used.

Topic Sentence 2: *Now I will talk about computers used in science.*

Analysis: Like the faulty "announcer" thesis statement, this "announcer" topic sentence is vague and merely names the topic.

Topic Sentence 3: *First, computers used in science have improved our lives.*

Analysis: The transition word *First* helps link the introduction and this paragraph. It adds unity to the essay. It does not, however, give specifics about the improvement computers have made in our lives.

Topic Sentence 4: *First used in scientific research and spaceflights, computers are now used extensively in the diagnosis and treatment of disease.*

Analysis: This sentence is the most thorough and fluent. It provides specific areas that will be discussed in the paragraph and offers more than an announcement of the topic. The writer gives concrete information about the content of the paragraph that will follow.

Summary Guidelines for Writing Topic Sentences
1. Specifically relate the topic to the thesis statement.
2. State clearly and concretely the subject of the paragraph
3. Provide some transition from the previous paragraph
4. Avoid topic sentences that are facts, questions, or announcers.

See also Skill 2.2.

Skill 5.3 Recognize distracting details or material not relevant to the main idea of a paragraph or passage

The main idea of a passage may contain a wide variety of supporting information, but it is important that each sentence be related to the main idea. When a sentence contains information that bears little or no connection to the main idea, it is said to be **irrelevant**.

The following passage has several irrelevant sentences that are highlighted in bold

The New City Planning Committee is proposing a new capitol building to represent the multicultural face of New City. **The current mayor is a Democrat.** The new capitol building will be on 10th street across from the grocery store and next to the Recreational Center. It will be within walking distance to the subway and bus depot, as the designers want to emphasize the importance of public transportation. Aesthetically, the building will have a contemporary design featuring a brushed-steel exterior and large, floor to ceiling windows. **It is important for employees to have a connection with the outside world even when they are in their offices.** Inside the building, the walls will be moveable. This will not only facilitate a multitude of creative floor plans, but it will also create a focus on open communication and flow of information. **It sounds a bit gimmicky to me.** Finally, the capitol will feature a large outdoor courtyard full of lush greenery and serene fountains. **Work will now seem like Club Med to those who work at the New City capitol!**

Skill 5.4   **Recognize sentence fragments and run-on sentences**

Fragments

Fragments occur (1) if word groups standing alone are missing either a subject or a verb, and (2) if word groups containing a subject and verb and standing alone are actually made dependent because of the use of subordinating conjunctions or relative pronouns.

Error: The teacher waiting for the class to complete the assignment.

Problem: This sentence is not complete because an ing word alone does not function as a verb. When a helping verb is added (for example, was waiting), it will become a sentence.

Correction: *The teacher was waiting for the class to complete the assignment.*

Error: Until the last toy was removed from the floor.

Problem: Words such as until, because, although, when, and if make a clause dependent and thus incapable of standing alone. An independent clause must be added to make the sentence complete.

Correction: *Until the last toy was removed from the floor, the kids could not go outside to play.*

Error: The city will close the public library. Because of a shortage of funds.

Problem: The problem is the same as above. The dependent clause must be joined to the independent clause.

Correction: *The city will close the public library because of a shortage of funds.*

RACTICE EXERCISE – FRAGMENTS

Choose the option that corrects the underlined portion(s)of the sentence.
If no error exists, choose "No change is necessary."

1) Despite the lack of funds in the <u>budget it</u> was necessary to rebuild the roads that were damaged from the recent floods.

A) budget: it
B) budget, it
C) budget; it
D) No change is necessary.

2) After determining that the fire was caused by faulty <u>wiring, the</u> building inspector said the construction company should be fined.

A) wiring. The
B) wiring the
C) wiring; the
D) No change is necessary.

3) Many years after buying a grand <u>piano Henry</u> decided he'd rather play the violin instead.

A) piano: Henry
B) piano, Henry
C) piano; Henry
D) No change is necessary.

4) Computers are being used more and more <u>frequently. because</u> of their capacity to store information.

A) frequently because
B) frequently, because
C) frequently; because
D) No change is necessary.

5) Doug washed the floors <u>every day. to</u> keep them clean for the guests.

A) every day to
B) every day,
C) every day;
D) No change is necessary.

ANSWER KEY: PRACTICE EXERCISE FOR FRAGMENTS

1. B   The clause that begins with *despite* is independent and must be separated with the clause that follows by a comma. Option A is incorrect because a colon is used to set off a list or to emphasize what follows. In Option B, a comma incorrectly suggests that the two clauses are dependent.

2. D   In the test item, a comma correctly separates the dependent clause *After...wiring* at the beginning of the sentence from the independent clause that follows. Option A incorrectly breaks the two clauses into separate sentences, while Options B omits the comma, and Option C incorrectly suggests that the phrase is an independent clause.

3. B   The *phrase Henry decided...instead* must be joined to the independent clause. Option A incorrectly puts a colon before *Henry decided*, and Option C incorrectly separates the phrase as if it were an independent clause.

4. A   The second clause *because...information* is dependent and must be joined to the first independent clause. Option B is incorrect because as the dependent clause comes at the end of the sentence, rather than at the beginning, a comma is not necessary. In Option C, a semi-colon incorrectly suggests that the two clauses are independent.

5. A   The second clause *to keep...guests* is dependent and must be joined to the first independent clause. Option B is incorrect because as the dependent clause comes at the end of the sentence, rather than at the beginning, a comma is not necessary. In Option C, a semi-colon incorrectly suggests that the two clauses are independent.

Run-on sentences and comma splices

Comma splices appear when two sentences are joined by only a comma. Fused sentences appear when two sentences are run together with no punctuation at all.

Error: Dr. Sanders is a brilliant scientist, his research on genetic disorders won him a Nobel Prize.

Problem: A comma alone cannot join two independent clauses (complete sentences). The two clauses can be joined by a semi-colon, or they can be separated by a period.

Correction: *Dr. Sanders is a brilliant scientist; his research on genetic disorders won him a Nobel Prize.*

OR

Dr. Sanders is a brilliant scientist. His research on genetic disorders won him a Nobel Prize.

Error: Florida is noted for its beaches they are long, sandy, and beautiful.

Problem: The first sentence ends with the word beaches, and the second sentence cannot be joined with the first. The fused sentence error can be corrected in several ways: (1) one clause may be made dependent on another with a subordinating conjunction or a relative pronoun; (2) a semi-colon may be used to combine two equally important ideas; (3) the two independent clauses may be separated by a period.

Correction: *Florida is noted for its beaches, which are long, sandy, and beautiful.*

OR

Florida is noted for its beaches; they are long, sandy, and beautiful.

OR

Florida is noted for its beaches. They are long, sandy, and beautiful.

Error: The number of hotels has increased, however, the number of visitors has grown also.

Problem: The first sentence ends with the word increased, and a comma is not strong enough to connect it to the second sentence. The adverbial transition however does not function the same way as a coordinating conjunction and cannot be used with commas to link two sentences. Several different corrections are available.

Correction: *The number of hotels has increased; however, the number of visitors has grown also.*
[Two separate but closely related sentences are created with the use of the semicolon.]

OR

The number of hotels has increased. However, the number of visitors has grown also.
[Two separate sentences are created.]

OR

Although the number of hotels have increased, the number of visitors has grown also.
[One idea is made subordinate to the other and separated with a comma.]

OR

The number of hotels have increased, but the number of visitors has grown also.
[The comma before the coordinating conjunction *but* is appropriate. The adverbial transition however does not function the same way as the coordinating conjunction but does.]

PRACTICE EXERCISE – FUSED SENTENCES AND COMMA SPLICES

Choose the option that corrects an error in the underlined portion(s). If no error exists, choose "No change is necessary".

1)   Scientists are excited at the ability to clone a <u>sheep; however,</u> it is not yet known if the same can be done to humans.

   A) sheep, however,
   B) sheep. However,
   C) sheep, however;
   D) No change is necessary.

2)   Because of the rising cost of college <u>tuition the</u> federal government now offers special financial assistance, <u>such as loans,</u> to students.

   A) tuition, the
   B) tuition; the
   C) such as loans
   D) No change is necessary.

3)   As the number of homeless people continue to <u>rise, the major cities</u> like <u>New York and Chicago,</u> are now investing millions of dollars in low-income housing.

   A) rise. The major cities
   B) rise; the major cities
   C) New York and Chicago
   D) No change is necessary.

4)   Unlike in <u>the 1950's, most</u> households find the husband and wife working full-time to make <u>ends meet in many</u> different career fields.

   A) the 1950's; most
   B) the 1950's most
   C) ends meet, in many
   D) No change is necessary.

ANSWER KEY : PRACTICE EXERCISE FOR COMMA SPLICES AND FUSED SENTENCES

1) B   Option B correctly separates two independent clauses. The comma in Option A after the word sheep creates a run-on sentence. .The semi-colon in Option C does not separate the two clauses but occurs at an inappropriate point.

2) A   The comma in Option A correctly separates the independent clause and the dependent clause. .The semi-colon in Option B is incorrect because one of the clauses is independent.. Option C requires a comma to prevent a run-on sentence.

3) C   Option C is correct because a comma creates a run-on. .Option A is incorrect because the first clause is dependent. .The semi-colon in Option B incorrectly divides the dependent clause from the independent clause.

4) D   Option D correctly separates the two clauses with a comma. Option A incorrectly uses a semi-colon to divide the clauses. The lack of a comma in Option B creates a run-on sentence. Option C puts a comma in an inappropriate place.

Skill 5.5 **Demonstrate the ability to edit written text to improve grammar, sentence structure, and word usage**

Techniques to Maintain Focus

- **Focus on a main point.** The point should be clear to readers, and all sentences in the paragraph should relate to it.

- **Start the paragraph with a topic sentence.** This should be a general, one-sentence summary of the paragraph's main point, relating both toward the thesis and toward the content of the paragraph. (A topic sentence is sometimes unnecessary if the paragraph continues a developing idea clearly introduced in a preceding paragraph, or if the paragraph appears in a narrative of events where generalizations might interrupt the flow of the story.)

- **Stick to the point.** Eliminate sentences that do not support the topic sentence.

- **Be flexible.** If there is not enough evidence to support the claim your topic sentence is making, do not fall into the trap of wandering or introducing new ideas within the paragraph. Either find more evidence, or adjust the topic sentence to collaborate with the evidence that is available.

Techniques for revising written texts to achieve clarity and economy of expression

Enhancing Interest:

- Start out with an attention-grabbing introduction. This sets an engaging tone for the entire piece and will be more likely to pull the reader in.
- Use dynamic vocabulary and varied sentence beginnings. Keep the reader on their toes. If they can predict what you are going to say next, switch it up.
- Avoid using clichés (as cold as ice, the best thing since sliced bread, nip it in the bud). These are easy shortcuts, but they are not interesting, memorable, or convincing.

Ensuring Understanding:

- Avoid using the words, "clearly," "obviously," and "undoubtedly." Often, things that are clear or obvious to the author are not as apparent to the reader. Instead of using these words, make your point so strongly that it is clear on its own.
- Use the word that best fits the meaning you intend for, even if they are longer or a little less common. Try to find a balance, a go with a familiar yet precise word.
- When in doubt, explain further.

Revision of sentences to eliminate wordiness, ambiguity, and redundancy

Sometimes this exercise is seen by students as simply catching errors in spelling or word use. Students need to reframe their thinking about revising and editing. Some questions that need to be asked:

- Is the reasoning coherent?
- Is the point established?
- Does the introduction make the reader want to read this discourse?
- What is the thesis? Is it proven?
- What is the purpose? Is it clear? Is it useful, valuable, interesting?
- Is the style of writing so wordy that it exhausts the reader and interferes with engagement?
- Is the writing so spare that it is boring?
- Are the sentences too uniform in structure?
- Are there too many simple sentences?
- Are too many of the complex sentences the same structure?
- Are the compounds truly compounds or are they unbalanced?
- Are parallel structures truly parallel?
- If there are characters, are they believable?
- If there is dialogue, is it natural or stilted?
- Is the title appropriate?
- Does the writing show creativity or is it boring?
- Is the language appropriate? Is it too formal? Too informal? If jargon is used, is it appropriate?

Studies have clearly demonstrated that the most fertile area in teaching writing is this one. If students can learn to revise their own work effectively, they are well on their way to becoming effective, mature writers. Word processing is an important tool for teaching this stage in the writing process. Microsoft Word has tracking features that make the revision exchanges between teachers and students more effective than ever before.

COMPETENCY 6.0   UNDERSTAND THE PROPER USE OF SPELLING, PUNCTUATION, AND CAPITALIZATION IN STANDARD AMERICAN ENGLISH

Skill 6.1   Identify and correcting errors in spelling

Spelling correctly is not always easy, because English not only utilizes an often inconsistent spelling system but also uses many words derived from other languages. Good spelling is important because incorrect spelling damages the physical appearance of writing and may puzzle your reader.

The following words are misspelled the most often.

1. commitment
2. succeed
3. necessary
4. connected
5. opportunity
6. embarrassed
7. occasionally
8. receive
9. their
10. accelerate
11. patience
12. obstinate
13. achievement
14. responsibility
15. prejudice
16. familiar
17. hindrance
18. controversial
19. publicity
20. prescription
21. possession
22. accumulate
23. hospitality
24. judgment
25. conscious

26. height
27. leisurely
28. shield
29. foreign
30. innovative
31. similar
32. proceed
33. contemporary
34. beneficial
35. attachment
36. guarantee
37. tropical
38. misfortune
39. particular
40. yield

Spelling plurals and possessives

The multiplicity and complexity of spelling rules based on phonics, letter doubling, and exceptions to rules - not mastered by adulthood - should be replaced by a good dictionary. As spelling mastery is also difficult for adolescents, our recommendation is the same. Learning the use of a dictionary and thesaurus will be a more rewarding use of time.

Most plurals of nouns that end in hard consonants or hard consonant sounds followed by a silent *e* are made by adding *s*. Some words ending in vowels only add *s*.

> fingers, numerals, banks, bugs, riots, homes, gates, radios, bananas

Nouns that end in soft consonant sounds *s, j, x, z, ch,* and *sh,* add *es*. Some nouns ending in *o* add es.

> dresses, waxes, churches, brushes, tomatoes, potatoes

Nouns ending in *y* preceded by a vowel just add *s*.

> boys, alleys

Nouns ending in *y* preceded by a consonant change the *y* to *i* and add *es*.

> babies, corollaries, frugalities, poppies

Some nouns plurals are formed irregularly or remain the same.

> sheep, deer, children, leaves, oxen

Some nouns derived from foreign words, especially Latin, may make their plurals in two different ways - one of them Anglicized. Sometimes, the meanings are the same; other times, the two plurals are used in slightly different contexts. It is always wise to consult the dictionary.

> appendices, appendixes   criterion, criteria
> indexes, indices   crisis, crises

Make the plurals of closed (solid) compound words in the usual way except for words ending in *ful* which make their plurals on the root word.

> timelines, hairpins, cupsful

Make the plurals of open or hyphenated compounds by adding the change in inflection to the word that changes in number.

fathers-in-law, courts-martial, masters of art, doctors of medicine

Make the plurals of letters, numbers, and abbreviations by adding *s*.

fives and tens, IBMs, 1990s, *p*s and *q*s (Note that letters are italicized.)

I before E

i before e	grieve, fiend, niece, friend
except after c	receive, conceive, receipt
or when sounded like "a"	as in reindeer and weight, and reign
Exceptions:	weird, foreign, seize, leisure

Test on ei/ie words

Circle the correct spelling of the word in each parenthesis.

1. The (shield, shield) protected the gladiator from serious injury.
2. Tony (received, recieved) an award for his science project.
3. Our (neighbors, nieghbors), the Thomsons, are in the Witness Protection Program.
4. Janet's (friend, freind), Olivia, broke her leg while running the marathon.
5. She was unable to (conceive, concieve) a child after her miscarriage.
6. Rudolph the Red-Nosed (Riendeer, Reindeer) is my favorite Christmas song.
7. The farmer spent all day plowing his (feild, field).
8. Kat's (wieght, weight) loss plan failed, and she gained twenty pounds!
9. They couldn't (beleive, believe) how many people showed up for the concert.
10. Ruby's (niece, neice) was disappointed when the movie was sold out.

ANSWER KEY: EI/IE WORDS

1. shield
2. received
3. neighbors
4. friend
5. conceive
6. reindeer
7. field
8. weight
9. believe
10. niece

PRACTICE EXERCISE – SPELLING RULES

Add suffixes to the following words and write the correct spelling form in the blanks.

1) swing + ing   =   Swinging

2) use + able   =   useable x

3) choke + ing   =   choking ✓

4) furnish + ed   =   furnished ✓

5) punish + ment   =   punishment ✓

6) duty + ful   =   dutyful ✓

7) bereave + ment   =   bereavement ✓

8) shovel + ing   =   Shoveling ✓

9) argue + ment   =   argument ✓

10) connect + ed   =   connected ✓

11) remember + ed   =   remembered ✓

12) treat + able   =   treatable ✓

13) marry + s   =   marries ✓

14) recycle + able   =   recyclable ✓

15) waste + ful   =   wasteful ✓

16) pray + ing   =   praying ✓

17) reconstruct + ing   =   reconstructing ✓

18) outrage + ous   =   outrageous

ANSWER KEY: SPELLING RULES PRACTICE

1) swinging
2) useable
3) choking
4) furnished
5) punishment
6) dutiful
7) bereavement
8) shoveling
9) argument
10) connected
11) remembered
12) treatable
13) marries
14) recyclable
15) wasteful
16) praying
17) reconstructing
18) outrageous

Skill 6.2   Identifying and correcting errors in punctuation

Commas

Commas indicate a brief pause. They are used to set off dependent clauses and long introductory word groups, to separate words in a series, to set off unimportant material that interrupts the flow of the sentence, and to separate independent clauses joined by conjunctions.

Error: After I finish my master's thesis I plan to work in Chicago.

Problem: A comma is needed after an introductory dependent word-group containing a subject and verb.

Correction: *After I finish my master's thesis, I plan to work in Chicago.*

Error: I washed waxed and vacuumed my car today.

Problem: Nouns, phrases, or clauses in a list, as well as two or more coordinate adjectives that modify one word should be separated by commas. Although the word *and* is sometimes considered optional, it is often necessary to clarify the meaning.

Correction: *I washed, waxed, and vacuumed my car today.*

Error: She was a talented dancer but she is mostly remembered for her singing ability.

Problem: A comma is needed before a conjunction that joins two independent clauses (complete sentences).

Correction: *She was a talented dancer, but she is mostly remembered for her singing ability.*

Error: This incident is I think typical of what can happen when the community remains so divided.

Problem: Commas are needed between nonessential words or words that interrupt the main clause.

Correction: *This incident is, I think, typical of what can happen when the community remains so divided.*

Semicolons and colons

Semicolons are needed to separate two or more closely related independent clauses when the second clause is introduced by a transitional adverb. (These clauses may also be written as separate sentences, preferably by placing the adverb within the second sentence). **Colons** are used to introduce lists and to emphasize what follows.

Error: I climbed to the top of the mountain, it took me three hours.

Problem: A comma alone cannot separate two independent clauses. Instead a semicolon is needed to separate two related sentences.

Correction: *I climbed to the top of the mountain; it took me three hours.*

Error: In the movie, asteroids destroyed Dallas, Texas, Kansas City, Missouri, and Boston, Massachusetts.

Problem: Semicolons are needed to separate items in a series that already contains internal punctuation.

Correction: *In the movie, asteroids destroyed Dallas, Texas; Kansas City, Missouri; and Boston, Massachusetts.*

Error: Essays will receive the following grades, A for excellent, B for good, C for average, and D for unsatisfactory.

Problem: A colon is needed to emphasize the information or list that follows.

Correction: *Essays will receive the following grades: A for excellent, B for good, C for average, and D for unsatisfactory.*

Error: The school carnival included: amusement rides, clowns, food booths, and a variety of games.

Problem: The material preceding the colon and the list that follows is not a complete sentence. Do not separate a verb (or preposition) from the object.

Correction: *The school carnival included amusement rides ,clowns, food booths, and a variety of games.*

Apostrophes

Apostrophes are used to show either contractions or possession.

Error: She shouldnt be permitted to smoke cigarettes in the building.

Problem: An apostrophe is needed in a contraction in place of the missing letter.

Correction: *She shouldn't be permitted to smoke cigarettes in the building.*

Error: My cousins motorcycle was stolen from his driveway.

Problem: An apostrophe is needed to show possession.

Correction: *My cousin's motorcycle was stolen from his driveway.* (Note: The use of the apostrophe before the letter "s" means that there is just one cousin. The plural form would read the following way: My cousins' motorcycle was stolen from their driveway.)

Error: The childrens new kindergarten teacher was also a singer.

Problem: An apostrophe is needed to show possession.

Correction: (Note: Because the word children is already plural, the apostrophe and s must be added afterward to show ownership.)

Error: Children screams could be heard for miles.

Problem: An apostrophe and the letter s are needed in the sentence to show whose screams it is.

Correction: *Children's screams could he heard for miles.* (Note: Because the word children is already plural, the apostrophe and s must be added afterward to show ownership.)

Quotation marks

In a quoted statement that is either declarative or imperative, place the period inside the closing quotation marks.

"The airplane crashed on the runway during takeoff."

If the quotation is followed by other words in the sentence, place a comma inside the closing quotations marks and a period at the end of the sentence.

"The airplane crashed on the runway during takeoff," said the announcer.

In most instances in which a quoted title or expression occurs at the end of a sentence, the period is placed before either the single or double quotation marks.

"The middle school readers were unprepared to understand Bryant's poem 'Thanatopsis.'"

Early book-length adventure stories like *Don Quixote* and *The Three Musketeers* were known as "picaresque novels."

There is an instance in which the final quotation mark would precede the period—if the content of the sentence were about a speech or quote so that the understanding of the meaning would be confused by the placement of the period.

The first thing out of his mouth was "Hi, I'm home."

but

The first line of his speech began "I arrived home to an empty house".

In sentences that are interrogatory or exclamatory, the question mark or exclamation point should be positioned outside the closing quotation marks if the quote itself is a statement or command or cited title.

Who decided to lead us in the recitation of the "Pledge of Allegiance"?

Why was Tillie shaking as she began her recitation, "Once upon a midnight dreary..."?

I was embarrassed when Mrs. White said, "Your slip is showing"!

In sentences that are declarative but the quotation is a question or an exclamation, place the question mark or exclamation point inside the quotation marks.

> The hall monitor yelled, "Fire! Fire!"
> "Fire! Fire!" yelled the hall monitor.

> Cory shrieked, "Is there a mouse in the room?" (In this instance, the question supersedes the exclamation.)

Quotations - whether words, phrases, or clauses - should be punctuated according to the rules of the grammatical function they serve in the sentence.

> The works of Shakespeare, "the bard of Avon," have been contested as originating with other authors.

> "You'll get my money," the old man warned, "when 'Hell freezes over'."

> Sheila cited the passage that began "Four score and seven years ago..." (Note the ellipsis followed by an enclosed period.)

> "Old Ironsides" inspired the preservation of the U.S.S. Constitution.

Use quotation marks to enclose the titles of shorter works: songs, short poems, short stories, essays, and chapters of books. (See "Using Italics" for punctuating longer titles.)

> "The Tell-Tale Heart"   "Casey at the Bat"   "America the Beautiful"

Dashes and Italics

Place **dashes** to denote sudden breaks in thought.

> Some periods in literature - the Romantic Age, for example - spanned different time periods in different countries.

Use dashes instead of commas if commas are already used elsewhere in the sentence for amplification or explanation.

> The Fireside Poets included three Brahmans - James Russell Lowell, Henry David Wadsworth, Oliver Wendell Holmes - and John Greenleaf Whittier.

Use **italics** to punctuate the titles of long works of literature, names of periodical publications, musical scores, works of art and motion picture television, and radio programs. (When unable to write in italics, students should be instructed to underline in their own writing where italics would be appropriate.)

The Idylls of the King   *Hiawatha*   *The Sound and the Fury*
Mary Poppins   *Newsweek*   *The Nutcracker Suite*

Skill 6.3   Identify and correcting errors in capitalization

Capitalize all proper names of persons (including specific organizations or agencies of government); places (countries, states, cities, parks, and specific geographical areas); and things (political parties, structures, historical and cultural terms, and calendar and time designations); and religious terms (any deity, revered person or group, sacred writings).

Percy Bysshe Shelley, Argentina, Mount Rainier National Park, Grand Canyon, League of Nations, the Sears Tower, Birmingham, Lyric Theater, Americans, Midwesterners, Democrats, Renaissance, Boy Scouts of America, Easter, God, Bible, Dead Sea Scrolls, Koran

Capitalize proper adjectives and titles used with proper names.

California gold rush, President John Adams, French fries, Homeric epic, Romanesque architecture, Senator John Glenn

Note: Some words that represent titles and offices are not capitalized unless used with a proper name.

Capitalized	Not Capitalized
Congressman McKay	the congressman from Florida
Commander Alger	commander of the Pacific Fleet
Queen Elizabeth	the queen of England

Capitalize all main words in titles of works of literature, art, and music.

Error: Emma went to Dr. Peters for treatment since her own Doctor was on vacation.

Problem: The use of capital letters with Emma and Dr .Peters is correct since they are specific (proper) names; the title Dr. is also capitalized. However, the word doctor is not a specific name and should not be capitalized.

Correction: *Emma went to Dr. Peters for treatment since her own doctor was on vacation.*

Error: Our Winter Break does not start until next wednesday.

Problem: Days of the week are capitalized, but seasons are not capitalized.

Correction: *Our winter break does not start until next Wednesday.*

Error: The exchange student from israel who came to study biochemistry spoke spanish very well.

Problem: Languages and the names of countries are always capitalized. Courses are also capitalized when they refer to a specific course; they are not capitalized when they refer to courses in general.

Correction: *The exchange student from Israel who came to study Biochemistry spoke Spanish very well.*

PRACTICE EXERCISE – CAPITALIZATION AND PUNCTUALIZATION

Choose the option that corrects an error in the underlined portion(s). If no error exists, choose "No change is necessary".

1) <u>Greenpeace</u> is an <u>Organization</u> that works to preserve the <u>world's</u> environment.

    A) greenpeace
    B) organization
    C) worlds
    D) No change is necessary.

2) When our class travels to <u>France</u> next <u>year, we</u> will see the <u>country's</u> many famous landmarks.

    A) france
    B) year; we
    C) countries
    D) No change is necessary.

3) <u>New York City</u>, the heaviest populated city <u>in America has</u> more than eight million people living there <u>everyday</u>.

    A) new york city
    B) in America, has
    C) Everyday
    D) No change is necessary.

4) The <u>television</u> show The X-Files has gained a huge <u>following because</u> it focuses on paranormal phenomena, extraterrestrial life, and the oddities of <u>human existence</u>.

    A) Television
    B) following, because
    C) Human existence
    D) No change is necessary.

5) Being a <u>Policeman</u> requires having many <u>qualities:</u> physical <u>agility,</u> good reflexes, and the ability to make quick decisions.

    A) policeman
    B) qualities;
    C) agility:
    D) No change is necessary.

ANSWER KEY: PRACTICE EXERCISE FOR CAPITALIZATION AND PUNCTUATION

1. B   In the sentence, the word organization does not need to be capitalized, due to the fact that it is a general noun. In Option A, the name of the organization should be capitalized. In Option C, the apostrophe is used to show that one world is being protected, not more than one.

2. D   In Option A, France is capitalized because it is the name of a country. In Option B, the comma, not the semi-colon, should separate a dependent clause from the main clause. In Option C, the use of an apostrophe and an s indicates only one country is being visited.

3. B   In Option A, New York City is capitalized because it is the name of a place. In Option B, a comma is needed to separate the noun America, from the verb has. In Option C, the noun everyday needs no capitalization.

4. D   In Option A, television does not need to be capitalized because it is a noun. In Option B, a comma is necessary to separate an independent clause from the main clause. In Option C, human existence is a general term that does not need capitalization.

5. A   In Option A, policeman does not need capitalization because it is a general noun. In Option B, a colon, not a semi-colon, is needed because the rest of the sentence is related to the main clause. In Option C, a comma, not a colon, is needed to separate the adjectives.

Sample Test: Writing

DIRECTIONS : *The passage below contains many errors. Read the passage. Then answer each test item by choosing the option that corrects an error in the underlined portion(s). No more than one underlined error will appear in each item. If no error exists, choose "No change is necessary."*

Climbing to the top of Mount Everest is an adventure. One which everyone--whether physically fit or not--seems eager to try. The trail stretches for miles, the cold temperatures are usually frigid and brutal.

Climbers must endure severel barriers on the way, including other hikers, steep jagged rocks, and lots of snow. Plus, climbers often find the most grueling part of the trip is their climb back down, just when they are feeling greatly exhausted. Climbers who take precautions are likely to find the ascent less arduous than the unprepared. By donning heavy flannel shirts, gloves, and hats, climbers prevented hypothermia, as well as simple frostbite. A pair of rugged boots is also one of the necesities. If climbers are to avoid becoming dehydrated, there is beverages available for them to transport as well.

Once climbers are completely ready to begin their lengthy journey, they can comfortable enjoy the wonderful scenery. Wide rock formations dazzle the observers eyes with shades of gray and white, while the peak forms a triangle that seems to touch the sky. Each of the climbers are reminded of the splendor and magnifisence of Gods great Earth.

1. **Climbing to the top of Mount Everest is an adventure. One which everyone —whether physically fit or not— seems eager to try.**

    A. adventure, one
    B. people, whether
    C. seem
    D. No change is necessary,

2. **The trail stretches for miles, the cold temperatures are usually frigid and brutal.**

    A. trails
    B. miles;
    C. usual
    D. No change is necessary,

3. **Climbers must endure severel barriers on the way, including other hikers, steep jagged rocks, and lots of snow.**

    A. several
    B. on the way: including
    C. hikers'
    D. No change is necessary,

4. Plus, climbers often find the most grueling part of the trip is <u>their</u> climb back <u>down, just</u> when they <u>are</u> feeling greatly exhausted.

A. his
B. down; just
C. were
D. No change is necessary.

5. <u>Climbers who</u> take precautions are likely to find the ascent <u>less difficult than</u> the unprepared.

A. Climbers, who
B. least difficult
C. then
D. No change is necessary.

6. By donning heavy flannel shirts, boots, and <u>hats, climbers prevented</u> hypothermia, as well as simple frostbite.

A. hats climbers
B. can prevent
C. hypothermia;
D. No change is necessary.

7. A pair of rugged boots <u>is also one</u> of the <u>necesities</u>.

A. are
B. also, one
C. necessities
D. No change is necessary.

8. If climbers are to avoid <u>becoming</u> dehydrated, there <u>is</u> beverages available for <u>them</u> to transport as well.

A. becomming
B. are
C. him
D. No change is necessary.

9. Once climbers are completely prepared for <u>their</u> lengthy <u>journey, they</u> can <u>comfortable</u> enjoy the wonderful scenery.

A. they're
B. journey; they
C. comfortably
D. No change is necessary.

10. Wide rock formations dazzle the <u>observers eyes</u> with shades of gray and <u>white, while</u> the peak <u>forms</u> a triangle that seems to touch the sky.

A. observers' eyes
B. white; while
C. formed
D. No change is necessary.

11. Each of the climbers <u>are</u> reminded of the splendor and <u>magnifisence</u> of <u>God's</u> great Earth.

A. is
B. magnifisence
C. Gods
D. No change is necessary.

DIRECTIONS: *The passage below contains several errors. Read the passage. Then answer each test item by choosing the option that corrects an error in the underlined portion(s). No more than one underlined error will appear in each item. If no error exists, choose "No change is necessary."*

Every job places different kinds of demands on their employees. For example, whereas such jobs as accounting and bookkeeping require mathematical ability; graphic design requires creative/artistic ability.

Doing good at one job does not usually guarantee success at another. However, one of the elements crucial to all jobs are especially notable: the chance to accomplish a goal.

The accomplishment of the employees varies according to the job. In many jobs the employees become accustom to the accomplishment provided by the work they do every day.

In medicine, for example, every doctor tests him self by treating badly injured or critically ill people. In the operating room, a team of Surgeons, is responsible for operating on many of these patients. In addition to the feeling of accomplishment that the workers achieve, some jobs also give a sense of identity to the employees'. Profesions like law, education, and sales offer huge financial and emotional rewards. Politicians are public servants: who work for the federal and state governments. President bush is basically employed by the American people to make laws and run the country.

Finally; the contributions that employees make to their companies and to the world cannot be taken for granted. Through their work, employees are performing a service for their employers and are contributing something to the world.

12. **Every job <u>places</u> different kinds of demands on <u>their employees</u>.**

    A. place
    B. its
    C. employes
    D. No change is necessary.

13. **<u>For example, whereas</u> such jobs as accounting and bookkeeping require mathematical <u>ability;</u> graphic design requires creative/artistic ability.**

    A. For example
    B. whereas,
    C. ability,
    D. No change is necessary.

14. **Doing <u>good</u> at one job does not <u>usually</u> guarantee <u>success</u> at another.**

    A. well
    B. usualy
    C. succeeding
    D. No change is necessary.

15. **However,** one of the elements crucial to all jobs **are** especially **notable:** the accomplishment of a goal.

   A. However
   B. is
   C. notable;
   D. No change is necessary.

16. The **accomplishment** of the **employees varies** according to the job.

   A. accomplishment,
   B. employee's
   C. vary
   D. No change is necessary.

17. In many jobs the employees **become accustom** to the accomplishment **provided** by the work they do every day.

   A. became
   B. accustomed
   C. provides
   D. No change is necessary.

18. In medicine, for example, every doctor **tests him self** by treating badly injured and critically ill people.

   A. test
   B. himself
   C. critical
   D. No change is necessary.

19. In the **operating room,** a team of **Surgeons, is** responsible for operating on many of **these** patients.

   A. operating room:
   B. surgeons is
   C. those
   D. No change is necessary.

20. In addition to the feeling of accomplishment that the workers **achieve,** some jobs also **give** a sense of self-identity to the **employees'.**

   A. acheive
   B. gave
   C. employees
   D. No change is necessary.

21. **Profesions** like law, **education,** and sales **offer** huge financial and emotional rewards.

   A. Professions
   B. education;
   C. offered
   D. No change is necessary.

22. Politicians **are** public **servants: who work** for the federal and state governments.

   A. were
   B. servants who
   C. worked
   D. No change is necessary.

23. **President bush is basically employed <u>by</u> the American people to <u>make</u> laws and run the country.**

   A. Bush
   B. to
   C. made
   D. No change is necessary .

24. **<u>Finally;</u> the contributions that employees make to <u>their</u> companies and to the world cannot be <u>taken</u> for granted.**

   A. Finally,
   B. their
   C. took
   D. No change is necessary.

DIRECTIONS: *For the underlined sentence(s), choose the option that expresses the meaning with the most fluency and the clearest logic within the context. If the underlined sentence should not be changed, choose Option A, which shows no change.*

25. **Selecting members of a President's cabinet can often be an aggravating process. <u>Either there are too many or too few qualified candidates for a certain position, and then they have to be confirmed by the Senate, where there is the possibility of rejection.</u>**

   A. Either there are too many or too few qualified candidate for a certain position, and then they have to be confirmed by the Senate, where there is the possibility of rejection.

   B. Qualified candidates for certain positions face the possibility of rejection, when they have to be confirmed by the Senate.

   C. The Senate has to confirm qualified candidates, who face the possibility of rejection.

   D. Because the Senate has to confirm qualified candidates; they face the possibility of rejection.

Answer Key: Writing

1. A	14. A
2. B	15. B
3. A	16. C
4. D	17. B
5. D	18. B
6. B	19. B
7. C	20. C
8. B	21. A
9. C	22. B
10. A	23. A
11. A	24. A
12. B	25. C
13. C	

Rationales for Sample Questions: Writing

1. **A** A comma is needed between *adventure* and *one* to avoid creating a fragment of the second part. In Option B, a comma after *everyone* would not be appropriate when the dash is used on the other side of *not*. In Option C, the singular verb *seems* is needed to agree with the singular subject *everyone*.

2. **B** A semicolon, not a comma, is needed to separate the first independent clause from the second independent clause. Option A is incorrect because the plural subject *trails* needs the singular verb *stretch*. Option C is incorrect because the adverb form *usually* is needed to modify the adjective *frigid*.

3. **A** The word *several* is misspelled in the text. Option B is incorrect because a comma, not a colon, is needed to set off the modifying phrase. Option C is incorrect because no apostrophe is needed after *hikers* since possession is not involved.

4. **D** The present tense must be used consistently throughout, therefore Option C is incorrect.   Option A is incorrect because the singular pronoun *his* does not agree with the plural antecedent *climbers*. Option B is incorrect because a comma, not a semicolon, is needed to separate the dependent clause from the main clause.

5. **D** No change is needed. Option A is incorrect because a comma would make the phrase *who take precautions* seem less restrictive or less essential to the sentence. Option B is incorrect because *less* is appropriate when two items--the prepared and the unprepared--are compared. Option C is incorrect because the comparative adverb *than*, not *then*, is needed.

6. **B** The verb *prevented* is in the past tense and must be changed to the present *can prevent* to be consistent. Option A is incorrect because a comma is needed after a long introductory phrase. Option C is incorrect because the semicolon creates a fragment of the phrase *as well as simple frostbite*.

7. **C** The word *necessities* is misspelled in the text. Option A is incorrect because the singular verb is must agree with the singular noun *pair* (a collective singular). Option B is incorrect because if *also* is set off with commas (potential correction), it should be set off on both sides.

8. **B** The plural verb *are* must be used with the plural subject *beverages*. Option A is incorrect because *becoming* has only one m. Option C is incorrect because the plural pronoun *them* is needed to agree with the referent *climbers*.

9. **C** The adverb form *comfortably* is needed to modify the verb phrase *can enjoy*. Option A is incorrect because the possessive plural pronoun is spelled *their*. Option B is incorrect because a semi-colon would make the first half of the item seem like an independent clause when the subordinating conjunction *once* makes that clause dependent.

10. **A** An apostrophe is needed to show the plural possessive form *observers' eyes*. Option B is incorrect because the semicolon would make the second half of the item seem like an independent clause when the subordinating conjunction *while* makes that clause dependent. Option C is incorrect because *formed* is in the wrong tense.

11. **A** The singular verb *is* agrees with the singular subject *each*. Option B is incorrect because *magnificence* is misspelled. Option C is incorrect because an apostrophe is needed to show possession.

12. **B** The singular possessive pronoun *its* must agree with its antecedent *job*, which is singular also. Option A is incorrect because *place* is a plural form and the subject, *job*, is singular. Option C is incorrect because the correct spelling of employees is given in the sentence.

13. **C** An introductory dependent clause is set off with a comma, not a semicolon. Option A is incorrect because the transitional phrase *for example* should be set off with a comma. Option B is incorrect because the adverb *whereas* functions like *while* and does not take a comma after it.

14. **A** The adverb *well* modifies the word *doing*. Option B is incorrect because *usually* is spelled correctly in the sentence. Option C is incorrect because *succeeding* is in the wrong tense.

15. **B** The singular verb *is* is needed to agree with the singular subject *one*. Option A is incorrect because a comma is needed to set off the transitional word *however*. Option C is incorrect because a colon, not a semicolon, is needed to set off an item.

16. **C** The singular verb *vary* is needed to agree with the singular subject *accomplishment*. Option A is incorrect because a comma after *accomplishment* would suggest that the modifying phrase of the employees is additional instead of essential. Option B is incorrect because employees is not possessive.

17. **B** The past participle *accustomed* is needed with the verb *become*. Option A is incorrect because the verb tense does not need to change to the past *became*. Option C is incorrect because *provides* is the wrong tense.

18. **B** The reflexive pronoun *himself* is needed. (Him self is nonstandard and never correct.) Option A is incorrect because the singular verb test is needed to agree with the singular subject doctor. Option C is incorrect because the adverb *critically* is needed to modify the verb *ill*.

19. **B** *Surgeons* is not a proper name so it does not need to be capitalized. A comma is not needed to break up a team of surgeons from the rest of the sentence. Option A is incorrect because a comma, not a colon, is needed to set off an item. Option C is incorrect because *those* is an incorrect pronoun.

20. **C** Option C is correct because *employees* is not possessive. Option A is incorrect because *achieve* is spelled correctly in the sentence. Option B is incorrect because *gave* is the wrong tense.

21. **A** Option A is correct because *professions* is misspelled in the sentence. Option B is incorrect because a comma, not a semi-colon, is needed after *education*. In Option C, *offered*, is in the wrong tense.

22. **B** A colon is not needed to set off the introduction of the sentence. In Option A, *were*, is the incorrect tense of the verb. In Option C, *worked*, is in the wrong tense.

23. **A** *Bush* is a proper name and should be capitalized. Option B, *to*, does not fit with the verb *employed*. Option C uses the wrong form of the verb, *make*.

24. **A** A comma is needed to separate *Finally* from the rest of the sentence. Finally is a preposition which usually heads a dependent sentence, hence a comma is needed. Option B is incorrect because *their* is misspelled. Option C is incorrect because *took* is the wrong form of the verb.

25. **C** Option C is the most straightforward and concise sentence. Option A is too unwieldy with the wordy *Either...or* phrase at the beginning. Option B doesn't make clear the fact that candidates face rejection by the Senate. Option D illogically implies that candidates face rejection because they have to be confirmed by

SUBAREA III.   MATHEMATICS

COMPETENCY 7.0   UNDERSTAND NUMBER SENSE AND BASIC ALGEBRA

Skill 7.1   Demonstrate the ability to perform basic addition, subtraction, multiplication, and division of whole numbers, fractions, and decimals

Whole numbers are natural numbers and zero.
        0, 1, 2, 3, ,4 ,5 ,6 ...

A **fraction** is an expression of numbers in the form of x/y, where x is the numerator and y is the denominator, which cannot be zero.

Example: $\dfrac{3}{7}$ 3 is the numerator; 7 is the denominator

If the fraction has common factors for the numerator and denominator, divide both by the common factor to reduce the fraction to its lowest form.

Example:

$$\frac{13}{39} = \frac{1 \times 13}{3 \times 13} = \frac{1}{3}$$ Divide by the common factor 13

Decimals = deci = part of ten. To find the decimal equivalent of a fraction, use the denominator to divide the numerator as shown in the following example.

Example: Find the decimal equivalent of $\dfrac{7}{10}$.
            Since 10 cannot divide into 7 evenly
$$\frac{7}{10} = 0.7$$

Rational numbers can be expressed as the ratio of two integers, $\dfrac{a}{b}$ where $b \neq 0$, for example $\dfrac{2}{3}$, $-\dfrac{4}{5}$, $5 = \dfrac{5}{1}$.

The rational numbers include integers, fractions and mixed numbers, terminating and repeating decimals. Every rational number can be expressed as a repeating or terminating decimal and can be shown on a number line.

Integers are positive and negative whole numbers and zero.

...-6, -5, -4, -3, -2, -1, 0, 1, 2, 3, 4, 5, 6, ...

Whole numbers are natural numbers and zero.

0, 1, 2, 3, ,4 ,5 ,6 ...

Natural numbers are the counting numbers.

1, 2, 3, 4, 5, 6, ...

Irrational numbers are real numbers that cannot be written as the ratio of two integers. These are infinite non-repeating decimals.

Examples: $\sqrt{5} = 2.2360..$, pi $= \Pi = 3.1415927...$

A **fraction** is an expression of numbers in the form of x/y, where *x* is the numerator and *y* is the denominator, which cannot be zero.

Example: $\frac{3}{7}$ 3 is the numerator; 7 is the denominator

If the fraction has common factors for the numerator and denominator, divide both by the common factor to reduce the fraction to its lowest form.

Example:

$$\frac{13}{39} = \frac{1 \times 13}{3 \times 13} = \frac{1}{3}$$ Divide by the common factor 13

A **mixed** number has an integer part and a fractional part.

Example: $2\frac{1}{4}, \ ^{-}5\frac{1}{6}, \ 7\frac{1}{3}$

Percent = per 100 (written with the symbol %). Thus 10% $= \frac{10}{100} = \frac{1}{10}$.

Decimals = deci = part of ten. To find the decimal equivalent of a fraction, use the denominator to divide the numerator as shown in the following example.

Example: Find the decimal equivalent of $\frac{7}{10}$.

Since 10 cannot divide into 7 evenly

$$\frac{7}{10} = 0.7$$

Addition of whole numbers

Example: At the end of a day of shopping, a shopper had $24 remaining in his wallet. He spent $45 on various goods. How much money did the shopper have at the beginning of the day?

The total amount of money the shopper started with is the sum of the amount spent and the amount remaining at the end of the day.

$$\begin{array}{r} 24 \\ +\ 45 \\ \hline 69 \end{array}$$ → The original total was $69.

Example: A race took the winner 1 hr. 58 min. 12 sec. on the first half of the race and 2 hr. 9 min. 57 sec. on the second half of the race. How much time did the entire race take?

        1 hr. 58 min. 12 sec.
      + 2 hr. 9 min. 57 sec.   Add these numbers
        3 hr. 67 min. 69 sec.
      + 1 min -60 sec.   Change 60 seconds to 1
                                    min.
        3 hr. 68 min. 9 sec.
      + 1 hr.-60 min.   .   Change 60 minutes to 1 hr.
        4 hr. 8 min. 9 sec. ←final answer

Subtraction of Whole Numbers

Example: At the end of his shift, a cashier has $96 in the cash register. At the beginning of his shift, he had $15. How much money did the cashier collect during his shift?

The total collected is the difference of the ending amount and the starting amount.

$$\begin{array}{r} 96 \\ -\ 15 \\ \hline 81 \end{array}$$ → The total collected was $81.

Multiplication of whole numbers

Multiplication is one of the four basic number operations. In simple terms, multiplication is the addition of a number to itself a certain number of times. For example, 4 multiplied by 3 is the equal to 4 + 4 + 4 or 3 + 3 + 3 +3. Another way of conceptualizing multiplication is to think in terms of groups. For example, if we have 4 groups of 3 students, the total number of students is 4 multiplied by 3. We call the solution to a multiplication problem the product.

The basic algorithm for whole number multiplication begins with aligning the numbers by place value with the number containing more places on top.

$$\begin{array}{r} 172 \\ \times\ 43 \\ \hline \end{array}$$ → Note that we placed 122 on top because it has more places than 43 does.

Next, we multiply the ones' place of the second number by each place value of the top number sequentially.

$$\begin{array}{r} (2) \\ 172 \\ \times\ 43 \\ \hline 516 \end{array}$$ → {3 x 2 = 6, 3 x 7 = 21, 3 x 1 = 3}
Note that we had to carry a 2 to the hundreds' column because 3 x 7 = 21. Note also that we add, not multiply, carried numbers to the product.

Next, we multiply the number in the tens' place of the second number by each place value of the top number sequentially. Because we are multiplying by a number in the tens' place, we place a zero at the end of this product.

$$\begin{array}{r} (2) \\ 172 \\ \times\ 43 \\ \hline 516 \\ 6880 \end{array}$$ → {4 x 2 = 8, 4 x 7 = 28, 4 x 1 = 4}

Finally, to determine the final product we add the two partial products.

$$\begin{array}{r} 172 \\ \times\ 43 \\ \hline 516 \\ +\ 6880 \\ \hline 7396 \end{array}$$ → The product of 172 and 43 is 7396.

Example: A student buys 4 boxes of crayons. Each box contains 16 crayons. How many total crayons does the student have?

The total number of crayons is 16 x 4.

$$
\begin{array}{r}
16 \\
\times\ 4 \\
\hline
64
\end{array}
$$
→ Total number of crayons equals 64.

Division of whole numbers

Division, the inverse of multiplication, is another of the four basic number operations. When we divide one number by another, we determine how many times we can multiply the divisor (number divided by) before we exceed the number we are dividing (dividend). For example, 8 divided by 2 equals 4 because we can multiply 2 four times to reach 8 (2 x 4 = 8 or 2 + 2 + 2 + 2 = 8). Using the grouping conceptualization we used with multiplication, we can divide 8 into 4 groups of 2 or 2 groups of 4. We call the answer to a division problem the quotient.

If the divisor does not divide evenly into the dividend, we express the leftover amount either as a remainder or as a fraction with the divisor as the denominator. For example, 9 divided by 2 equals 4 with a remainder of 1 or 4 ½.

The basic algorithm for division is long division. We start by representing the quotient as follows.

$14\overline{)293}$ → 14 is the divisor and 293 is the dividend. This represents 293 ÷ 14.

Next, we divide the divisor into the dividend starting from the left.

$14\overline{)293}$ with 2 above → 14 divides into 29 two times with a remainder.

Next, we multiply the partial quotient by the divisor, subtract this value from the first digits of the dividend, and bring down the remaining dividend digits to complete the number.

$$
\begin{array}{r}
2 \\
14\overline{)293} \\
-28 \\
\hline
13
\end{array}
$$
→ 2 x 14 = 28, 29 – 28 = 1, and bringing down the 3 yields 13.

Finally, we divide again (the divisor into the remaining value) and repeat the preceding process. The number left after the subtraction represents the remainder.

$$14\overline{)293}$$

quotient 20
$$- 28$$
$$\quad 13$$
$$- 0$$
$$\quad 13$$

The final quotient is 20 with a remainder of 13. We can also represent this quotient as 20 13/14.

Example: Each box of apples contains 24 apples. How many boxes must a grocer purchase to supply a group of 252 people with one apple each?

The grocer needs 252 apples. Because he must buy apples in groups of 24, we divide 252 by 24 to determine how many boxes he needs to buy.

$$24\overline{)252}$$

10
$$-24$$
$$\quad 12$$
$$- 0$$
$$\quad 12$$

The quotient is 10 with a remainder of 12.

Thus, the grocer needs 10 boxes plus 12 more apples. Therefore, the minimum number of boxes the grocer can purchase is 11.

Example: At his job, John gets paid $20 for every hour he works. If John made $940 in a week, how many hours did he work?

This is a division problem. To determine the number of hours John worked, we divide the total amount made ($940) by the hourly rate of pay ($20). Thus, the number of hours worked equals 940 divided by 20.

$$20\overline{)940}$$

47
$$-80$$
$$\quad 140$$
$$-140$$
$$\quad\quad 0$$

20 divides into 940, 47 times with no remainder.

John worked 47 hours.

Addition and Subtraction of Decimals

When adding and subtracting decimals, we align the numbers by place value as we do with whole numbers. After adding or subtracting each column, we bring the decimal down, placing it in the same location as in the numbers added or subtracted.

Example: Find the sum of 152.3 and 36.342.

$$
\begin{array}{r}
152.300 \\
+\quad 36.342 \\
\hline
188.642
\end{array}
$$

Note that we placed two zeroes after the final place value in 152.3 to clarify the column addition.

Example: Find the difference of 152.3 and 36.342.

$$
\begin{array}{cc}
\overset{2\ 9\ 10}{152.\cancel{300}} & \overset{(4)11(12)}{1\cancel{52}.\cancel{300}} \\
-\quad 36.342 & -\quad 36.342 \\
\hline
58 & 115.958
\end{array}
$$

Note how we borrowed to subtract from the zeroes in the hundredths' and thousandths' place of 152.300.

Multiplication of Decimals

When multiplying decimal numbers, we multiply exactly as with whole numbers and place the decimal moving in from the left the total number of decimal places contained in the two numbers multiplied. For example, when multiplying 1.5 and 2.35, we place the decimal in the product 3 places in from the left (3.525).

Example: Find the product of 3.52 and 4.1.

$$
\begin{array}{r}
3.52 \\
\times\quad 4.1 \\
\hline
352 \\
+\quad 14080 \\
\hline
14432
\end{array}
$$

Note that there are 3 total decimal places in the two numbers.

We place the decimal 3 places in from the left.

Thus, the final product is 14.432.

Example: A shopper has 5 one-dollar bills, 6 quarters, 3 nickels, and 4 pennies in his pocket. How much money does he have?

$$5 \times \$1.00 = \$5.00 \qquad \begin{array}{r} \overset{3}{\$0.25} \\ \times\ 6 \\ \hline \$1.50 \end{array} \qquad \begin{array}{r} \$0.05 \\ \times\ 3 \\ \hline \$0.15 \end{array} \qquad \begin{array}{r} \$0.01 \\ \times\ 4 \\ \hline \$0.04 \end{array}$$

Note the placement of the decimals in the multiplication products. Thus, the total amount of money in the shopper's pocket is:

$$\begin{array}{r} \$5.00 \\ 1.50 \\ 0.15 \\ +\ 0.04 \\ \hline \$6.69 \end{array}$$

Division of Decimals

When dividing decimal numbers, we first remove the decimal in the divisor by moving the decimal in the dividend the same number of spaces to the right. For example, when dividing 1.45 into 5.3 we convert the numbers to 145 and 530 and perform normal whole number division.

Example: Find the quotient of 5.3 divided by 1.45.
            Convert to 145 and 530.

Divide.

$$\begin{array}{r} 3 \\ 145\overline{)530} \\ -\ 435 \\ \hline 95 \end{array} \longrightarrow \begin{array}{r} 3.65 \\ 145\overline{)530.00} \\ -\ 435 \\ \hline 950 \\ -\ 870 \\ \hline 800 \end{array} \longrightarrow$$ Note that we insert the decimal to continue division.

Because one of the numbers divided contained one decimal place, we round the quotient to one decimal place. Thus, the final quotient is 3.7.

Operating with Percents

Example: 5 is what percent of 20?

This is the same as converting $\dfrac{5}{20}$ to % form.

$$\frac{5}{20} \times \frac{100}{1} = \frac{5}{1} \times \frac{5}{1} = 25\%$$

Example: There are 64 dogs in the kennel. 48 are collies. What percent are collies?

Restate the problem.   48 is what percent of 64?
Write an equation. $48 = n \times 64$
Solve. $\dfrac{48}{64} = n$

$n = \dfrac{3}{4} = 75\%$

75% of the dogs are collies.

Example: The auditorium was filled to 90% capacity. There were 558 seats occupied. What is the capacity of the auditorium?

Restate the problem.   90% of what number is 558?
Write an equation. $0.9n = 558$
Solve. $n = \dfrac{558}{.9}$
                         $n = 620$

The capacity of the auditorium is 620 people.

Example: A pair of shoes costs $42.00. Sales tax is 6%. What is the total cost of the shoes?

Restate the problem.   What is 6% of 42?
Write an equation. $n = 0.06 \times 42$
Solve. $n = 2.52$

Add the sales tax to the cost. $42.00 + $2.52 = $44.52

The total cost of the shoes, including sales tax, is $44.52.

Addition and subtraction of fractions

<u>Key Points</u>

1. You need a common denominator in order to add and subtract reduced and improper fractions.

   Example: $\dfrac{1}{3} + \dfrac{7}{3} = \dfrac{1+7}{3} = \dfrac{8}{3} = 2\dfrac{2}{3}$

   Example: $\dfrac{4}{12} + \dfrac{6}{12} - \dfrac{3}{12} = \dfrac{4+6-3}{12} = \dfrac{7}{12}$

2. Adding an integer and a fraction of the <u>same</u> sign results directly in a mixed fraction.

   Example: $2 + \dfrac{2}{3} = 2\dfrac{2}{3}$

   Example: $^{-}2 - \dfrac{3}{4} = ^{-}2\dfrac{3}{4}$

3. Adding an integer and a fraction with different signs involves the following steps.

   -get a common denominator
   -add or subtract as needed
   -change to a mixed fraction if possible

   Example: $2 - \dfrac{1}{3} = \dfrac{2 \times 3 - 1}{3} = \dfrac{6-1}{3} = \dfrac{5}{3} = 1\dfrac{2}{3}$

   Example: Add $7\dfrac{3}{8} + 5\dfrac{2}{7}$

   Add the whole numbers; add the fractions and combine the two results:

   $7\dfrac{3}{8} + 5\dfrac{2}{7} = (7+5) + (\dfrac{3}{8} + \dfrac{2}{7})$

   $= 12 + \dfrac{(7 \times 3) + (8 \times 2)}{56}$ (LCM of 8 and 7)

   $= 12 + \dfrac{21+16}{56} = 12 + \dfrac{37}{56} = 12\dfrac{37}{56}$

Example: Perform the operation.

$$\frac{2}{3} - \frac{5}{6}$$

We first find the LCM of 3 and 6 which is 6.

$$\frac{2 \times 2}{3 \times 2} - \frac{5}{6} \rightarrow \frac{4-5}{6} = \frac{^-1}{6} \qquad \text{(Using method A)}$$

Example:

$$^-7\frac{1}{4} + 2\frac{7}{8}$$

$$^-7\frac{1}{4} + 2\frac{7}{8} = (^-7 + 2) + (\frac{^-1}{4} + \frac{7}{8})$$

$$= (^-5) + \frac{(^-2 + 7)}{8} = (^-5) + (\frac{5}{8})$$

$$= (^-5) + \frac{5}{8} = \frac{^-5 \times 8}{1 \times 8} + \frac{5}{8} = \frac{^-40 + 5}{8}$$

$$= \frac{^-35}{8} = ^- 4\frac{3}{8}$$

Divide 35 by 8 to get 4, remainder 3.

Caution: Common error would be

$$^-7\frac{1}{4} + 2\frac{7}{8} = ^-7\frac{2}{8} + 2\frac{7}{8} = ^- 5\frac{9}{8} \qquad \text{Wrong.}$$

It is correct to add -7 and 2 to get -5, but adding $\frac{2}{8} + \frac{7}{8} = \frac{9}{8}$

is wrong. It should have been $\frac{^-2}{8} + \frac{7}{8} = \frac{5}{8}$. Then,

$$^-5 + \frac{5}{8} = ^- 4\frac{3}{8} \quad \text{as before.}$$

Multiplication of fractions

Using the following example: $3\dfrac{1}{4}\times\dfrac{5}{6}$

1. Convert each number to an improper fraction.

$$3\dfrac{1}{4}=\dfrac{(12+1)}{4}=\dfrac{13}{4}\qquad \dfrac{5}{6}\text{ is already in reduced form.}$$

2. Reduce (cancel) common factors of the numerator and denominator if they exist.

$$\dfrac{13}{4}\times\dfrac{5}{6}\quad\text{No common factors exist.}$$

3. Multiply the numerators by each other and the denominators by each other.

$$\dfrac{13}{4}\times\dfrac{5}{6}=\dfrac{65}{24}$$

4. If possible, reduce the fraction back to its lowest term.

$$\dfrac{65}{24}\quad\text{Cannot be reduced further.}$$

5. Convert the improper fraction back to a mixed fraction by using long division.

$$\dfrac{65}{24}=24\overline{)65}\;\dfrac{2}{}\quad\begin{array}{r}48\\\hline17\end{array}\quad=2\dfrac{17}{24}$$

Summary of sign changes for multiplication:

a. $(+)\times(+)=(+)$

b. $(-)\times(+)=(-)$

c. $(+)\times(-)=(-)$

d. $(-)\times(-)=(+)$

Example:

$$7\frac{1}{3} \times \frac{5}{11} = \frac{22}{3} \times \frac{5}{11}$$

Reduce like terms (22 and 11)

$$= \frac{2}{3} \times \frac{5}{1} = \frac{10}{3} = 3\frac{1}{3}$$

Example:

$$-6\frac{1}{4} \times \frac{5}{9} = \frac{-25}{4} \times \frac{5}{9}$$

$$= \frac{-125}{36} = -3\frac{17}{36}$$

Example:

$$\frac{-1}{4} \times \frac{-3}{7}$$

Negative times a negative equals positive.

$$= \frac{1}{4} \times \frac{3}{7} = \frac{3}{28}$$

Division of fractions:

1. Change mixed fractions to improper fraction.

2. Change the division problem to a multiplication problem by using the reciprocal of the number after the division sign.

3. Find the sign of the final product.

4. Cancel if common factors exist between the numerator and the denominator.

5. Multiply the numerators tcgether and the denominators together.

6. Change the improper fraction to a mixed number.

Example:

$$3\frac{1}{5} \div 2\frac{1}{4} = \frac{16}{5} \div \frac{9}{4}$$

$$= \frac{16}{5} \times \frac{4}{9}$$

Reciprocal of $\frac{9}{4}$ is $\frac{4}{9}$.

$$= \frac{64}{45} = 1\frac{19}{45}$$

Example:

$$7\frac{3}{4} \div 11\frac{5}{8} = \frac{31}{4} \div \frac{93}{8}$$

$$= \frac{31}{4} \times \frac{8}{93} \quad \text{Reduce like terms.}$$

$$= \frac{1}{1} \times \frac{2}{3} = \frac{2}{3}$$

Example:

$$\left(-2\frac{1}{2}\right) \div 4\frac{1}{6} = \frac{-5}{2} \div \frac{25}{6}$$

$$= \frac{-5}{2} \times \frac{6}{25} \quad \text{Reduce like terms.}$$

$$= \frac{-1}{1} \times \frac{3}{5} = \frac{-3}{5}$$

Example:

$$\left(-5\frac{3}{8}\right) \div \left(\frac{-7}{16}\right) = \frac{-43}{8} \div \frac{-7}{16}$$

$$= \frac{-43}{8} \times \frac{-16}{7} \quad \text{Reduce like terms.}$$

$$= \frac{43}{1} \times \frac{2}{7} \quad \text{Negative times a negative equals a positive.}$$

$$= \frac{86}{7} = 12\frac{2}{7}$$

Skill 7.2 Demonstrate knowledge of the correct order of operations

The Order of Operations are to be followed when evaluating algebraic expressions. Follow these steps in order:

1. Simplify inside grouping characters such as parentheses, brackets, square root, fraction bar, etc.

2. Multiply out expressions with exponents.

3. Do multiplication or division, from left to right.

4. Do addition or subtraction, from left to right.

Example:

$$3^3 - 5(b+2)$$

$$= 3^3 - 5b - 10$$

$$= 27 - 5b - 10 = 17 - 5b$$

Example:

$$2 - 4 \times 2^3 - 2(4 - 2 \times 3)$$

$$= 2 - 4 \times 2^3 - 2(4-6) = 2 - 4 \times 2^3 - 2(^-2)$$

Skill 7.3 Recognize and interpreting mathematical symbols (e.g., +, –, <, >, ≤, ≥)

Symbol for inequality: In the symbol '>' (greater than) or '<' (less than), the big open side of the symbol always faces the larger of the two numbers and the point of the symbol always faces the smaller number.

Example: Compare 15 and 20 on the number line.

Since 20 is further away from the zero than 15 is, then 20 is greater than 15, or $20 > 15$.

Example: Compare $\dfrac{3}{7}$ and $\dfrac{5}{10}$.

To compare fractions, they should have the same least common denominator (LCD). The LCD in this example is 70.

$$\frac{3}{7} = \frac{3 \times 10}{7 \times 10} = \frac{30}{70} \qquad\qquad \frac{5}{10} = \frac{5 \times 7}{10 \times 7} = \frac{35}{70}$$

Since the denominators are equal, compare only the denominators. $30 < 35$, so:

$$\frac{3}{7} < \frac{5}{10}$$

Skill 7.4   **Demonstrate knowledge of definitions of basic terms such as sum, difference, product, quotient, numerator, and denominator**

Sum –   The result of adding two numbers.

For Example: 12 + 6 = 18

Difference –   The result of subtracting two numbers.

For Example57 – 29 = 28

Product –   The result of two numbers being multiplied together.

For Example: 5 x 5 = 25

Quotient –   The result of dividing one number by another.

For Example: 32 / 8 = 4

Numerator –   The number above the bar in a fraction that tells how many equal parts of the whole are being considered

Denominator –   The number below the bar in a fraction that tells how many equal parts are in the whole

For Example: $\dfrac{3}{4}$ ← Numerator
                                    ← Denominator

Skill 7.5 **Recognize the relative positions of numbers on a number line (e.g., 13 is between 14 and 12) and equivalent forms of numbers (e.g., 12= .5)**

See Skill 7.3.

Skill 7.6 **Demonstrate knowledge of place value for whole numbers and decimal numbers**

Whole Number Place Value

Consider the number 792. We can assign a place value to each digit.

Reading from left to right, the first digit (7) represents the hundreds' place. The hundreds' place tells us how many sets of one hundred the number contains. Thus, there are 7 sets of one hundred in the number 792.

The second digit (9) represents the tens' place. The tens' place tells us how many sets of ten the number contains. Thus, there are 9 sets of ten in the number 792.

The last digit (2) represents the ones' place. The ones' place tells us how many ones the number contains. Thus, there are 2 sets of one in the number 792.

Therefore, there are 7 sets of 100, plus 9 sets of 10, plus 2 ones in the number 792.

Decimal Place Value

More complex numbers have additional place values to both the left and right of the decimal point. Consider the number 374.8.

Reading from left to right, the first digit (3) is in the hundreds' place and tells us the number contains 3 sets of one hundred.

The second digit (7) is in the tens' place and tells us the number contains 7 sets of ten.

The third digit, 4, is in the ones' place and tells us the number contains 4 ones.

Finally, the number after the decimal (8) is in the tenths' place and tells us the number contains 8 tenths.

Skill 7.7   Demonstrate the ability to solve problems (e.g., basic math operations and/or estimation)

To estimate measurement of familiar objects, it is first necessary to determine the units to be used.

<u>Examples:</u>
Length
1. The coastline of Florida
2. The width of a ribbon
3. The thickness of a book
4. The depth of water in a pool

Weight or mass
1. A bag of sugar
2. A school bus
3. A dime

Capacity or volume
1. Paint to paint a bedroom
2. Glass of milk

Money
1. Cost of a house
2. Cost of a cup of coffee
3. Exchange rate

Perimeter
1. The edge of a backyard
2. The edge of a football field

Area
1. The size of a carpet
2. The size of a state

Example: Estimate the measurements of the following objects:

Length of a dollar bill	6 inches
Weight of a baseball	1 pound
Distance from New York to Florida	1100 km
Volume of water to fill a medicine dropper	1 milliliter
Length of a desk	2 meters
Temperature of water in a swimming pool	80° F

Depending on the degree of accuracy needed, an object may be measured to different units. For example, a pencil may be 6 inches to the nearest inch, or 6 3 8 inches to the nearest eighth of an inch. Similarly, it might be 15 cm to the nearest cm or 154 mm to the nearest mm.

Given a set of objects and their measurements, the use of rounding procedures is helpful when attempting to round to the nearest given unit. When rounding to a given place value, it is necessary to look at the number in the next smaller place. If this number is 5 or more, the number in the place we are rounding to is increased by one and all numbers to the right are changed to zero. If the number is less than 5, the number in the place we are rounding to stays the same and all numbers to the right are changed to zero.

One method of rounding measurements can require an additional step. First, the measurement must be converted to a decimal number. Then the rules for rounding applied.

Example: Round the measurements to the given units.

MEASUREMENT	ROUND TO NEAREST	ANSWER
1 foot 7 inches	foot	2 ft
5 pound 6 ounces	pound	5 pounds
5 9/16 inches	inch	6 inches

Convert each measurement to a decimal number. Then apply the rules for rounding.

1 foot 7 inches = $1\frac{7}{12}$ ft = 1.58333 ft, round up to 2 ft

5 pounds 6 ounces = $5\frac{6}{16}$ pounds = 5.375 pound, round to 5 pounds

$5\frac{9}{16}$ inches = 5.5625 inches, round up to 6 inches

Example: Janet goes into a store to purchase a CD on sale for $13.95. While shopping, she sees two pairs of shoes, prices $19.95 and $14.50. She only has $50. Can she purchase everything?

Solve by rounding:

$19.95→$20.00
$14.50→$15.00
$13.95→$14.00
       $49.00   Yes, she can purchase the CD and the shoes.

Skill 7.8 **Demonstrate the ability to solve a single-step equation involving one variable (e.g., find *x* if *x* + 3 = 5)**

Procedure for solving algebraic equations

Example: $3(x+3) = ^-2x+4$ Solve for *x*.
1)   Expand to eliminate all parentheses.

$$3x+9 = ^-2x+4$$

2)   Multiply each term by the LCD to eliminate all denominators.

3)   Combine like terms on each side when possible.

4)   Use the properties to put all variables on one side and all constants on the other side.

$$\rightarrow 3x+9-9 = ^-2x+4-9 \quad \text{(subtract nine from both sides)}$$

$$\rightarrow 3x = ^-2x-5$$

$$\rightarrow 3x+2x = ^-2x+2x-5 \quad \text{(add 2x to both sides)}$$

$$\rightarrow 5x = ^-5$$

$$\rightarrow \frac{5x}{5} = \frac{^-5}{5} \quad \text{(divide both sides by 5)}$$

$$\rightarrow x = ^-1$$

Example: Solve: $3(2x+5)-4x = 5(x+9)$

$$6x+15-4x = 5x+45$$
$$2x+15 = 5x+45$$
$$^-3x+15 = 45$$
$$^-3x = 30$$
$$x = ^-10$$

Example: Mark and Mike are twins. Three times Mark's age plus four equals four times Mike's age minus 14. How old are the boys?

Since the boys are twins, their ages are the same. "Translate" the English into Algebra. Let x = their age

$3x + 4 = 4x - 14$

$18 = x$

The boys are each 18 years old.

Example: The YMCA wants to sell raffle tickets to raise $32,000. If they must pay $7,250 in expenses and prizes out of the money collected from the tickets, how many tickets worth $25 each must they sell?

Let x = number of tickets sold
Then $25x$ = total money collected for x tickets

Total money minus expenses is greater than $32,000.

$25x - 7250 = 32,000$
$25x = 39350$
$x = 1570$

If they sell 1,570 tickets, they will raise $32,000.

Example: The Simpsons went out for dinner. All 4 of them ordered the aardvark steak dinner. Bert paid for the 4 meals and included a tip of $12 for a total of $84.60. How much was an aardvark steak dinner?

Let x = the price of one aardvark dinner.
So $4x$ = the price of 4 aardvark dinners.

Skill 7.9   Demonstrate the ability to compute percentages

Percent means per 100 (%).

Example: 10 percent $= \dfrac{10}{100} = \dfrac{1}{10} = 0.1$

Example: 10 percent of 150 means $\dfrac{10}{100} \times \dfrac{150}{1} = 15$

Example: Add 75% of 25 to 10% of 1000.

75% of 25 $= \dfrac{75}{100} \times \dfrac{25}{1} = \dfrac{75}{4} \times \dfrac{1}{1} = \dfrac{75}{4} = 18\dfrac{3}{4}$ and

10% of 1000 $= \dfrac{10}{100} \times \dfrac{1000}{1} = \dfrac{10}{1} \times \dfrac{10}{1} = 100$

Adding the two numbers gives:

$18\dfrac{3}{4} + 100 = 118\dfrac{3}{4}$ or 118.75

Example: 5 is what percent of 20?

This is the same as converting $\dfrac{5}{20}$ to % form.

$\dfrac{5}{20} \times \dfrac{100}{1} = \dfrac{5}{1} \times \dfrac{5}{1} = 25\%$

Example: An item on sale at 75% discount is now sold for $12.50. What was the selling price before the sale?

$12.50 is 75% of the price. What was full price?

$\dfrac{12.50}{75} \times \dfrac{100}{1} = \dfrac{50}{3} = \$16.667 \approx \$16.67$

Example: There are 64 dogs in the kennel. 48 are collies. What percent are collies?

Restate the problem.   48 is what percent of 64?
Write an equation. $48 = n \times 64$

Solve. $\dfrac{48}{64} = n$

$n = \dfrac{3}{4} = 75\%$

75% of the dogs are collies.

Example: The auditorium was filled to 90% capacity. There were 558 seats occupied. What is the capacity of the auditorium?

Restate the problem.   90% of what number is 558?
Write an equation. $0.9n = 558$

Solve. $n = \dfrac{558}{.9}$

                            $n = 620$

The capacity of the auditorium is 620 people.

Example: A pair of shoes costs $42.00. Sales tax is 6%. What is the total cost of the shoes?

Restate the problem.   What is 6% of 42?
Write an equation. $n = 0.06 \times 42$
Solve. $n = 2.52$

Add the sales tax to the cost. $42.00 + $2.52 = $44.52

The total cost of the shoes, including sales tax, is $44.52.

**COMPETENCY 8.0   UNDERSTAND BASIC CONCEPTS OF GEOMETRY
                   AND MEASUREMENT**

**Skill 8.1   Demonstrate the ability to represent time and money in more
              than one way (e.g., 15 minutes = 14 hour; 1:45 = quarter of
              eleven; $.25 = a quarter)**

Elapsed **time** problems are usually one of two types. One type of problem is the
elapsed time between 2 times given in hours, minutes, and seconds. The other
common type of problem is between 2 times given in months and years.

For any time of day past noon, change it into military time by adding 12 hours.
For instance, 1:15 p.m. would be 13:15. Remember when you borrow a minute or
an hour in a subtraction problem that you have borrowed 60 more seconds or
minutes.

Example: Find the time from 11:34:22 a.m. until 3:28:40 p.m.

First change 3:28:40 p.m. to   15:28:40 p.m.
Now subtract   - 11:34:22 a.m.
                                      :18
Borrow an hour and add 60 more minutes. Subtract
  14:88:40 p.m.
- 11:34:22 a.m.
    3:54:18 ↔ 3 hours, 54 minutes, 18 seconds

Example: A race took the winner 1 hr. 58 min. 12 sec. on the first half of the
            race and 2 hr. 9 min. 57 sec. on the second half of the race. How
            much time did the entire race take?

1 hr. 58 min. 12 sec.
+ 2 hr. 9 min. 57 sec.   Add these numbers
3 hr. 67 min. 69 sec
+ 1 min -60 sec.   Change 60 seconds to 1 min.
3 hr. 68 min. 9 sec.
+ 1 hr.-60 min.   .   Change 60 minutes to 1 hr.
4 hr. 8 min. 9 sec. ← final answer

Example: It takes Cynthia 45 minutes to get ready each morning. How many
            hours does she spend getting ready each week?

45 minutes X 7 days = 315 minutes

$$\frac{315 \text{ minutes}}{60 \text{ minutes in an hour}} \quad = \quad 5.25 \text{ hours}$$

Money

Example: Janet goes into a store to purchase a CD on sale for $13.95. While shopping, she sees two pairs of shoes, prices $19.95 and $14.50. She only has $50. Can she purchase everything?

Solve by rounding:

$19.95→$20.00
$14.50→$15.00
$13.95→<u>$14.00</u>
       $49.00   Yes, she can purchase the CD and the shoes.

Weight

Example: The weight limit of a playground merry-go-round is 1000 pounds.
There are 11 children on the merry-go-round.
3 children weigh 100 pounds.
6 children weigh 75 pounds
2 children weigh 60 pounds

George weighs 80 pounds. Can he get on the merry-go-round?

$3(100) + 6(75) + 2(60)$
$= 300 + 450 + 120$
$= 870$
$1000 - 870$
$= 130$

Since 80 is less than 130, George can get on the merry-go-round.

Skill 8.2 **Recognize techniques for converting between units of length, mass, volume, and weight in the same measurement system (e.g., feet to yards, milliliters to liters)**

Measurements of length (English system)

12 inches (in)	=	1 foot (ft)
3 feet (ft)	=	1 yard (yd)
1760 yards (yd)	=	1 mile (mi)

Measurements of length (Metric system)

kilometer (km)	=	1000 meters (m)
hectometer (hm)	=	100 meters (m)
decameter (dam)	=	10 meters (m)
meter (m)	=	1 meter (m)
decimeter (dm)	=	1/10 meter (m)
centimeter (cm)	=	1/100 meter (m)
millimeter (mm)	=	1/1000 meter (m)

Conversion of length from English to Metric

1 inch	=	2.54 centimeters
1 foot	≈	30 centimeters
1 yard	≈	0.9 meters
1 mile	≈	1.6 kilometers

Measurements of weight (English system)

28 grams (g)	=	1 ounce (oz)
16 ounces (oz)	=	1 pound (lb)
2000 pounds (lb)	=	1 ton (t)(short ton)
1.1 ton (t)	=	1 ton (t)

Measurements of weight (Metric system)

kilogram (kg)	=	1000 grams (g)
gram (g)	=	1 gram (g)
milligram (mg)	=	1/1000 gram (g)

Conversion of weight from English to metric

1 ounce	≈	28 grams
1 pound	≈	0.45 kilogram
	≈	454 grams

Measurement of volume (English system)

8 fluid ounces (oz)	=	1 cup (c)
2 cups (c)	=	1 pint (pt)
2 pints (pt)	=	1 quart (qt)
4 quarts (qt)	=	1 gallon (gal)

Measurement of volume (Metric system)

kiloliter (kl)	=	1000 liters (l)
liter (l)	=	1 liter (l)
milliliter (ml)	=	1/1000 liters (ml)

Conversion of volume from English to metric

1 teaspoon (tsp)	$\approx$	5 milliliters
1 fluid ounce	$\approx$	15 milliliters
1 cup	$\approx$	0.24 liters
1 pint	$\approx$	0.47 liters
1 quart	$\approx$	0.95 liters
1 gallon	$\approx$	3.8 liters

Measurement of time

1 second	=	
1 minute	=	60 seconds
1 hour	=	60 minutes
1 day	=	24 hours
1 week	=	7 days
1 year	=	365 days
1 century	=	100 years

Note: (') represents feet and (") represents inches.

Skill 8.3   Identify basic geometric figures (e.g., right triangle, cylinder, polygon)

Polygons, simple closed **two-dimensional figures** composed of line segments, are named according to the number of sides they have.

A **quadrilateral** is a polygon with four sides.
The sum of the measures of the angles of a quadrilateral is 360°.

A **trapezoid** is a quadrilateral with exactly <u>one</u> pair of parallel sides.

In an **isosceles trapezoid**, the non-parallel sides are congruent.

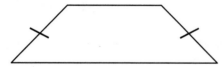

A **parallelogram** is a quadrilateral with <u>two</u> pairs of parallel sides.

In a parallelogram:
The diagonals bisect each other.
Each diagonal divides the parallelogram into two congruent triangles.
Both pairs of opposite sides are congruent.
Both pairs of opposite angles are congruent.
Two adjacent angles are supplementary.

A **rectangle** is a parallelogram with a right angle.

A **rhombus** is a parallelogram with all sides equal length.

A **square** is a rectangle with all sides equal length.

Example: True or false?

All squares are rhombuses.	True
All parallelograms are rectangles.	False - <u>some</u> parallelograms are rectangles
All rectangles are parallelograms.	True
Some rhombuses are squares.	True
Some rectangles are trapezoids.	False - only <u>one</u> pair of parallel sides
All quadrilaterals are parallelograms.	False -some quadrilaterals are parallelograms
Some squares are rectangles.	False - all squares are rectangles
Some parallelograms are rhombuses.	True

A **triangle** is a polygon with three sides.

Triangles can be classified by the types of angles or the lengths of their sides.

An **acute** triangle has exactly three *acute* angles.
A **right** triangle has one *right* angle.
An **obtuse** triangle has one *obtuse* angle.

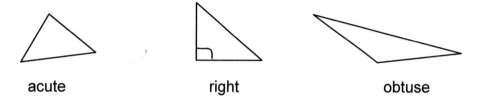

acute   right   obtuse

All *three* sides of an **equilateral** triangle are the same length.
Two sides of an **isosceles** triangle are the same length.
None of the sides of a **scalene** triangle are the same length.

equilateral   isosceles   scalene

Example: Can a triangle have two right angles?
             No. A right angle measures 90°, therefore the sum of two right
             angles would be 180° and there could not be third angle.

Example: Can a triangle have two obtuse angles?
             No. Since an obtuse angle measures more than 90° the sum of two
             obtuse angles would be greater than 180°.

A **cylinder** has two congruent circular bases that are parallel.

A **sphere** is a space figure having all its points the same distance from the center.

A **cone** is a space figure having a circular base and a single vertex.

A **pyramid** is a space figure with a square base and 4 triangle-shaped sides.

A **tetrahedron** is a 4-sided space triangle. Each face is a triangle.

A **prism** is a space figure with two congruent, parallel bases that are polygons.

Skill 8.4 **Demonstrate the ability to perform basic computations related to area, volume, and perimeter for basic geometric figures**

The **perimeter** of any polygon is the sum of the lengths of the sides.

The **area** of a polygon is the number of square units covered by the figure.

FIGURE	AREA FORMULA	PERIMETER FORMULA
Rectangle	LW	$2(L+W)$
Triangle	$\frac{1}{2}bh$	$a+b+c$
Parallelogram	bh	sum of lengths of sides
Trapezoid	$\frac{1}{2}h(a+b)$	sum of lengths of sides

Perimeter
Example: A farmer has a piece of land shaped as shown below. He wishes to fence this land at an estimated cost of $25 per linear foot. What is the total cost of fencing this property to the nearest foot.

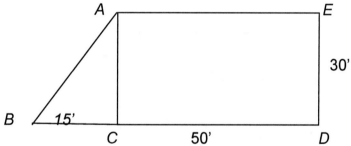

From the right triangle ABC, AC = 30 and BC = 15.

Since (AB) = (AC)^2 + (BC)^2
(AB) = (30)^2 + (15)^2

So $\sqrt{(AB)^2} = AB = \sqrt{1125} = 33.5410$ feet
To the nearest foot AB = 34 feet.

Perimeter of the piece of land is $= AB + BC + CD + DE + EA$

= 34 + 15 + 50 + 30 + 50 = 179 feet

cost of fencing = $25 x 179 = $4, 475.00

Area is the space that a figure occupies. Example:

Example: What will be the cost of carpeting a rectangular office that measures 12 feet by 15 feet if the carpet costs $12.50 per square yard?

12 ft

15 ft

The problem is asking you to determine the area of the office. The area of a rectangle is *length x width = A*
Substitute the given values in the equation *A = lw*

$A = (12 \text{ ft.})(15 \text{ ft.})$
$A = 180 \text{ ft.}$

The problem asked you to determine the cost of carpet at $12.50 per square yard.

First, you need to convert 180 ft.^{2} into yards^2.

$$1 \text{ yd.} = 3 \text{ ft.}$$
$$(1 \text{ yard})(1 \text{ yard}) = (3 \text{ feet})(3 \text{ feet})$$
$$1 \text{ yd}^2 = 9 \text{ ft } 2$$

Hence, $\dfrac{180 \text{ ft}^2}{1} = \dfrac{1 \text{ yd}^2}{9 \text{ ft}^2} = \dfrac{20}{1} = 20 \text{ yd}^2$

The carpet cost $12.50 per square yard; thus the cost of carpeting the office described is $12.50 x 20 = $250.00.

Example: Find the area of a parallelogram whose base is 6.5 cm and the height of the altitude to that base is 3.7 cm.

6.5 cm

3.7 cm

$A_{parallelogram}$ = bh

$$= (3.7)(6.5)$$
$$= 24.05 \text{ cm}^2$$

Example: Find the area of this triangle.

11.4 cm

9.3 cm   7.1 cm

16.8 cm

$A_{triangle} = \frac{1}{2} bh$
$$= 0.5\,(16.8)\,(7.1)$$
$$= 59.64 \text{ cm}^2$$

Example: Find the area of this trapezoid.

17.5 cm

6.4 cm

23.7 cm

The area of a trapezoid equals one-half the sum of the bases times the altitude.

$A_{trapezoid} = \frac{1}{2} h(b_1 + b_2)$
$$= 0.5\,(6.4)\,(17.5 + 23.7)$$
$$= 131.84 \text{ cm}^2$$

The distance around a circle is the **circumference**. The ratio of the circumference to the diameter is represented by the Greek letter pi. $\Pi \sim 3.14$ $\sim \dfrac{22}{7}$.

The circumference of a circle is found by the formula $C = 2\Pi r$ or $C = \Pi d$ where r is the radius of the circle and d is the diameter.

The **area** of a circle is found by the formula $A = \Pi r^2$.

Example: Find the circumference and area of a circle whose radius is 7 meters.

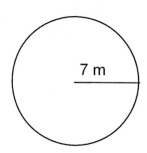

$C = 2\Pi r$

$= 2(3.14)(7)$

$= 43.96$ m

$A = \Pi r^2$

$= 3.14(7)(7)$

$= 153.86$ m^2

COMPETENCY 9.0   UNDERSTAND CONCEPTS RELATED TO DATA ANALYSIS

Skill 9.1   Demonstrate the ability to interpret and/or compare information from tables, charts, and graphs

To make a **bar graph** or a **pictograph**, determine the scale to be used for the graph. Then determine the length of each bar on the graph or determine the number of pictures needed to represent each item of information. Be sure to include an explanation of the scale in the legend.

Example: A class had the following grades:
4 A's, 9 B's, 8 C's, 1 D, 3 F's.
Graph these on a bar graph and a pictograph.

Pictograph

Grade	Number of Students
A	☺☺☺☺
B	☺☺☺☺☺☺☺☺☺
C	☺☺☺☺☺☺☺☺
D	☺
F	☺☺☺

Bar graph

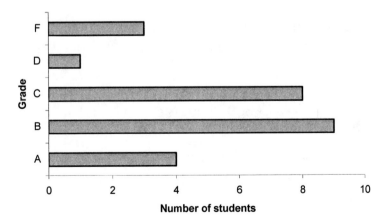

To make a **line graph**, determine appropriate scales for both the vertical and horizontal axes (based on the information to be graphed). Describe what each axis represents and mark the scale periodically on each axis. Graph the individual points of the graph and connect the points on the graph from left to right.

Example: Graph the following information using a line graph.

The number of National Merit finalists/school year

	90-91	91-92	92-93	93-94	94-95	95-96
Central	3	5	1	4	6	8
Wilson	4	2	3	2	3	2

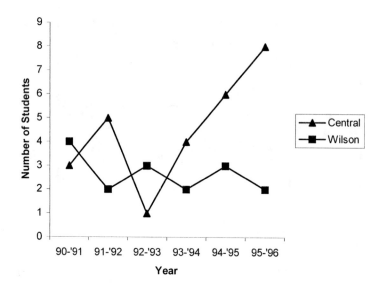

To make a **circle graph**, total all the information that is to be included on the graph. Determine the central angle to be used for each sector of the graph using the following formula:

$$\frac{\text{information}}{\text{total information}} \times 360^\circ = \text{degrees in central} \sphericalangle$$

Lay out the central angles to these sizes, label each section and include its percent.

Example: Graph this information on a circle graph:

Monthly expenses:

Rent, $400
Food, $150
Utilities, $75
Clothes, $75
Church, $100
Misc., $200

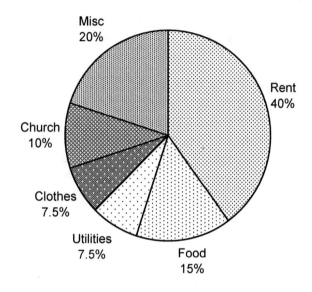

Scatter plots compare two characteristics of the same group of things or people and usually consist of a large body of data. They show how much one variable is affected by another. The relationship between the two variables is their **correlation**. The closer the data points come to making a straight line when plotted, the closer the correlation.

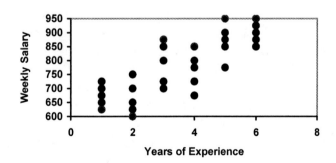

Stem and leaf plots are visually similar to line plots. The **stems** are the digits in the greatest place value of the data values, and the **leaves** are the digits in the next greatest place values. Stem and leaf plots are best suited for small sets of data and are especially useful for comparing two sets of data. The following is an example using test scores:

4	9
5	4 9
6	1 2 3 4 6 7 8 8
7	0 3 4 6 6 6 7 7 7 8 8 8 8
8	3 5 5 7 8
9	0 0 3 4 5
10	0 0

Histograms are used to summarize information from large sets of data that can be naturally grouped into intervals. The vertical axis indicates **frequency** (the number of times any particular data value occurs), and the horizontal axis indicates data values or ranges of data values. The number of data values in any interval is the **frequency of the interval**.

A **trend** line on a line graph shows the correlation between two sets of data. A trend may show positive correlation (both sets of data get bigger together) negative correlation (one set of data gets bigger while the other gets smaller), or no correlation.

An **inference** is a statement which is derived from reasoning. When reading a graph, inferences help with interpretation of the data that is being presented. From this information, a **conclusion** and even **predictions** about what the data actually means is possible.

Example: Katherine and Tom were both doing poorly in math class. Their teacher had a conference with each of them in November. The following graph shows their math test scores during the school year.

What kind of trend does this graph show?

This graph shows that there is a positive trend in Katherine's test scores and a negative trend in Tom's test scores.

What inferences can you make from this graph?

We can infer that Katherine's test scores rose steadily after November. Tom's test scores spiked in December but then began to fall again and became negatively trended.

What conclusion can you draw based upon this graph?

We can conclude that Katherine took her teacher's meeting seriously and began to study in order to do better on the exams. It seems as though Tom tried harder for a bit, but his test scores eventually slipped back down to the level where he began.

Skill 9.2   **Demonstrate the ability to determine the mean, median, and mode of a set of data**

The arithmetic **mean** (or average) of a set of numbers is the *sum* of the numbers given, *divided* by the number of items being averaged.

Example: Find the mean. Round to the nearest tenth.
24.6, 57.3, 44.1, 39.8, 64.5
The sum is 230.3 ˜ 5
= 46.06, rounded to 46.1

The **median** of a set is the middle number. To calculate the median, the terms must be arranged in order. If there are an even number of terms, the median is the mean of the two middle terms.

Example: Find the median.

12. 14. 27. 3. 13. 7. 17.   12. 22. 6.   16

Rearrange the terms. 16, 17, 22, 27
3, 6, 7, 12, 12, 13, 14,
Since there are 11 numbers, the middle would be the sixth number or 13.

The **mode** of a set of numbers is the number that occurs with the greatest frequency. A set can have no mode if each term appears exactly one time. Similarly, there can also be more than one mode.

Example: Find the mode.

26, 15, 37, **26**, 35, **26**, 15

15 appears twice, but 26 appears 3 times, therefore the mode is 26.

The **range** is the difference between the highest and lowest value of data items.

Example: Given the ungrouped data below, calculate the mean and range.

15	22	28	25	34	38
18	25	30	33	19	23

Mean $(\overline{X})$ = 25.8333333
Range: $38 - 15 = 23$

Skill 9.3   **Demonstrate the ability to represent data in graphic formats**

See Skill 9.1.

1. $\left(\dfrac{^-4}{9}\right) + \left(\dfrac{^-7}{10}\right) =$

   A. $\dfrac{23}{90}$

   B. $\dfrac{^-23}{90}$

   C. $\dfrac{103}{90}$

   D. $\dfrac{^-103}{90}$

2. $(5.6) \times (^-0.11) =$

   A. $^-0.616$

   B. 0.616

   C. $^-6.110$

   D. 6.110

3. Mary did comparison shopping on her favorite brand of coffee. Over half of the stores priced the coffee at $1.70. Most of the remaining stores priced the coffee at $1.80, except for a few who charged $1.90. Which of the following statements is true about the distribution of prices?

   A. The mean and the mode are the same.
   B. The mean is greater than the mode.
   C. The mean is less than the mode.
   D. The mean is less than the median.

4. $4\dfrac{2}{9} \times \dfrac{7}{10}$

   A. $4\dfrac{9}{10}$

   B. $\dfrac{266}{90}$

   C. $2\dfrac{43}{45}$

   D. $2\dfrac{6}{20}$

5. 0.74 =

A. $\dfrac{74}{100}$

B. 7.4%

C. $\dfrac{33}{50}$

D. $\dfrac{74}{10}$

6. $^-9\dfrac{1}{4}$ ☐ $^-8\dfrac{2}{3}$

A. =

B. <

C. >

D. ≤

7. 303 is what percent of 600?

A. 0.505%

B. 5.05%

C. 505%

D. 50.5%

8. An item that sells for $375 is put on sale at $120. What is the percent of decrease?

A. 25%

B. 28%

C. 68%

D. 34%

9. Given the formula $d = rt$, (where d = distance, r = rate, and t = time), calculate the time required for a vehicle to travel 585 miles at a rate of 65 miles per hour.

A. 8.5 hours

B. 6.5 hours

C. 9.5 hours

D. 9 hours

10. A restaurant employs 465 people. There are 280 waiters and 185 cooks. If 168 waiters and 85 cooks receive pay raises, what percent of the waiters will receive a pay raise?

A. 36.13%

B. 60%

C. 60.22%

D. 40%

11. Solve for x.

$$3x - \frac{2}{3} = \frac{5x}{2} + 2$$

A. $5\frac{1}{3}$

B. $\frac{17}{3}$

C. 2

D. $\frac{16}{2}$

12. The price of gas was $3.27 per gallon. Your tank holds 15 gallons of fuel. You are using two tanks a week. How much will you save weekly if the price of gas goes down to $2.30 per gallon

A. $26.00

B. $29.00

C. $15.00

D. $17.00

13. Which statement is true about George's budget?

A. George spends the greatest portion of his income on food.

B. George spends twice as much on utilities as he does on his mortgage.

C. George spends twice as much on utilities as he does on food.

D. George spends the same amount on food and utilities as he does on mortgage.

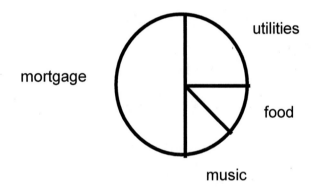

14. Round $1\frac{13}{16}$ of an inch to the nearest quarter of an inch.

A. $1\frac{1}{4}$ inch

B. $1\frac{5}{8}$ inch

C. $1\frac{3}{4}$ inch

D. 2 inches

15. The owner of a rectangular piece of land 40 yards in length and 30 yards in width wants to divide it into two parts. She plans to join two opposite corners with a fence as shown in the diagram below. The cost of the fence will be approximately $25 per linear foot. What is the estimated cost for the fence needed by the owner?

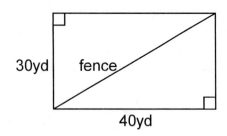

A. $1,250

B. $62,500

C. $5,250

D. $3,750

16. What measure could be used to report the distance traveled in walking around a track?

    A. degrees

    B. square meters

    C. kilometers

    D. cubic feet

17. What is the area of a square whose side is 13 feet?

    A. 169 feet

    B. 169 square feet

    C. 52 feet

    D. 52 square feet

18. The trunk of a tree has a 2.1 meter radius. What is its circumference?

    A. 2.1π square meters

    B. 4.2π meters

    C. 2.1π meters

    D. 4.2π square meters

19. The following chart shows the yearly average number of international tourists visiting Palm Beach for 1990-1994. How may more international tourists visited Palm Beach in 1994 than in 1991?

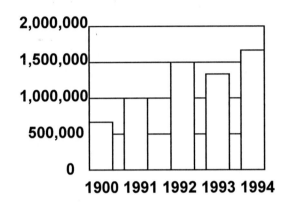

1900 1991 1992 1993 1994

    A.   100,000

    B.   600,000

    C.   1,600,000

    D.   8,000,000

20. Given $f(x) = (x)^3 - 3(x)^2 + 5$, find $x = (-2)$.

    A.   15

    B.   -15

    C.   25

    D.   -25

21. What type of triangle is $\triangle ABC$?

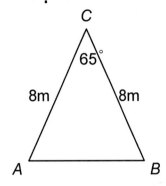

    A.   right

    B.   equilateral

    C.   scalene

    D.   isosceles

22. $\dfrac{7}{9} + \dfrac{1}{3} \div \dfrac{2}{3} =$

    A. $\dfrac{5}{3}$

    B. $\dfrac{3}{2}$

    C.   2

    D. $\dfrac{23}{18}$

23. What is the mode of the data in the following sample?

9, 10, 11, 9, 10, 11, 9, 13

A. 9

B. 9.5

C. 10

D. 11

24. Consider the graph of the distribution of the length of time it took individuals to complete an employment form.

Approximately how many individuals took less than 15 minutes to complete the employment form?

A. 35
B. 28
C. 7
D. 4

25. If $4x - (3 - x) = 7(x - 3) + 10$, then

A. $x = 8$

B. $x = -8$

C. $x = 4$

D. $x = -4$

Answer Key: Mathematics

1.	D		14.	C
2.	A		15.	D
3.	B		16.	C
4.	C		17.	B
5.	A		18.	B
6.	B		19.	B
7.	D		20.	B
8.	C		21.	D
9.	D		22.	D
10.	B		23.	A
11.	A		24.	C
12.	B		25.	C
13.	C			

Rationales for Sample Questions: Mathematics

1. Find the LCD of $\dfrac{^-4}{9}$ and $\dfrac{^-7}{10}$. The LCD is 90, so you get $\dfrac{^-40}{90}+\dfrac{^-63}{90}=\dfrac{^-103}{90}$, which is answer **D**.

2. Simple multiplication. The answer will be negative because a positive times a negative is a negative number. $5.6\times{^-}0.11={^-}0.616$, which is answer **A**.

3. Over half the stores priced the coffee at \$1.70, so this means that this is the mode. The mean would be slightly over \$1.70 because other stores priced the coffee at over \$1.70. Therefore, the answer is **B**.

4. Convert any mixed number to an improper fraction: $\dfrac{38}{9}\times\dfrac{7}{10}$. Since no common factors of numerators or denominators exist, multiply the numerators and the denominators by each other $=\dfrac{266}{90}$. Convert back to a mixed number and reduce $2\dfrac{86}{90}=2\dfrac{43}{45}$. The answer is **C**.

5. $0.74\rightarrow$ the 4 is in the hundredths place, so the answer is $\dfrac{74}{100}$, which is **A**.

6. The larger the absolute value of a negative number, the smaller the negative number is. The absolute value of $-9\dfrac{1}{4}$ is $9\dfrac{1}{4}$ which is larger than the absolute value of $-8\dfrac{2}{3}$ is $8\dfrac{2}{3}$. Therefore, the sign should be $-9\dfrac{1}{4}<-8\dfrac{2}{3}$, which is answer **B**.

7. Use x for the percent. $600x=303$. $\dfrac{600x}{600}=\dfrac{303}{600}\rightarrow x=0.505=50.5\%$, which is answer **D**.

8. Use $(1-x)$ as the discount. $375x=120$.
    $375(1-x)=120\rightarrow375-375x=120\rightarrow375x=255\rightarrow x=0.68=68\%$ which is answer **C**.

9. We are given $d=585$ miles and $r=65$ miles per hour and $d=rt$. Solve for t. $585=65t\rightarrow t=9$ hours, which is answer **D**.

10. The total number of waiters is 280 and only 168 of them get a pay raise. Divide the number getting a raise by the total number of waiters to get the percent. $\dfrac{168}{280} = 0.6 = 60\%$ which is answer **B.**

i. $6\left(\dfrac{1}{6}\right) \le 4\left(\dfrac{1}{6}\right)^2 + 2 = 1 \le 4\left(\dfrac{1}{36}\right) + 2 \to 1 \le \dfrac{1}{9} + 2 \to 1 \le 2\dfrac{1}{9}$ True.

11. $3x(6) - \dfrac{2}{3}(6) = \dfrac{5x}{2}(6) + 2(6)$ 6 is the LCD of 2 and 3

$18x - 4 = 15x + 12$

$18x = 15x + 16$

$3x = 16$

$x = \dfrac{16}{3} = 5\dfrac{1}{3}$ which is answer **A.**

12. 15 gallons x 2 tanks = 30 gallons a week
= 30 gallons x $3.27 = $98.10
30 gallons x $2.30 = $69.00
$98.10 - $69.00 = $29.10 is approximately $29.00. The answer is **B.**

13. George spends twice as much on utilities as he does on food; George spends twice as much on utilities as on food. **C.**

14. $1\dfrac{13}{16}$ inches is approximately $1\dfrac{12}{16}$, which is also $1\dfrac{3}{4}$, which is the nearest $\dfrac{1}{4}$ of an inch, so the answer is **C.**

15. Find the length of the diagonal by using the Pythagorean theorem. Let x be the length of the diagonal.

$30^2 + 40^2 = x^2 \to 900 + 1600 = x^2$

$2500 = x^2 \to \sqrt{2500} = \sqrt{x^2}$

$x = 50$ yards

Convert to feet. $\dfrac{50 \text{ yards}}{x \text{ feet}} = \dfrac{1 \text{ yard}}{3 \text{ feet}} \to 1500 \text{ feet}$

It cost $25.00 per linear foot, so the cost is (1500 ft)($25) = $3750, which is answer **D.**

16. Degrees measures angles, square meters measures area, cubic feet measure volume, and kilometers measures length. Kilometers is the only reasonable answer, which is **C.**

17. Area = length times width (*lw*).
Length = 13 feet
Width = 13 feet (square, so length and width are the same).
Area = $13 \times 13 = 169$ square feet.
Area is measured in square feet. So the answer is **B.**

18. Circumference is $2\pi r$, where r is the radius. The circumference is $2\pi 2.1 = 4.2\pi$ meters (not square meters because not measuring area), which is answer **B.**

19. The number of tourists in 1991 was 1,000,000 and the number in 1994 was 1,600,000. Subtract to get a difference of 600,000, which is answer **B.**

20. Substitute $x = -2$.

$f(-2) = (^-2)^3 - 3 \times (^-2)^2 + 5$

$f(-2) = {}^- 8 - 3(4) + 5$

$f(-2) = {}^- 8 - 12 + 5$

$f(-2) = {}^- 15$ The answer is **B.**

21. Two of the sides are the same length, so we know the triangle is either equilateral or isosceles. $\angle CAB$ and $\angle CBA$ are equal, because their sides are. Therefore, $180^\circ = 65^\circ - 2x = \dfrac{115^\circ}{2} = 57.5^\circ$. Because all three angles are not equal, the triangle is isosceles, so the answer is **D.**

22. First, do the division.

$\dfrac{1}{3} \div \dfrac{2}{3} = \dfrac{1}{3} \times \dfrac{3}{2} = \dfrac{1}{2}$

Add.

$\dfrac{7}{9} + \dfrac{1}{2} = \dfrac{14}{18} + \dfrac{9}{18} = \dfrac{23}{18}$, which is answer **D.**

23. The mode is the number that appears most frequently. 9 appears 3 times, which is more than the other numbers. Therefore the answer is **A.**

24. According to the chart, the number of people who took under 15 minutes is 7, which is answer **C.**

25. Solve for x.

$4x - (3 - x) = 7(x - 3) + 10$

$4x - 3 + x = 7x - 21 + 10$

$5x - 3 = 7x - 11$

$5x = 7x - 11 + 3$

$5x - 7x = {}^- 8$

$^- 2x = {}^- 8$

$x = 4$ The answer is **C.**

COMPETENCY 10.0   UNDERSTAND THE APPLICATION OF READING SKILLS TO CLASSROOM INSTRUCTION

Skill 10.1   Recognize elements of phonics (e.g., long and short vowels) and how words are formed (e.g., syllables, root words, prefixes, suffixes)

This aspect of vocabulary development is to help children look for structural elements within words which they can use independently to help them determine meaning.

Some teachers choose to directly teach structural analysis. In particular, those who teach by following the phonics-centered approach for reading do this. Other teachers, who follow the balanced literacy approach, introduce the structural components as part of mini lessons that are focused on the students' reading and writing.

Structural analysis of words as defined by J. David Cooper (2004) involves the study of significant word parts. This analysis can help the child with pronunciation and constructing meaning.

The term list below is generally recognized as the key structural analysis components.

Root Words- a word from which another word is developed. The second word can be said to have its "root" in the first. This structural component nicely lends itself to a tree with roots illustration which can make relevant the meaning for children. Children may also want to literally construct root words using cardboard trees and/or actual roots from plants to create word family models.

ELL learners can construct these models for their native language root word families, as well for the English language words they are learning. ELL learners in the 5th and 6th grade may even appreciate analyzing the different root structures for contrasts and similarities between their native language and English.

Special Needs learners can focus in small groups or individually with a paraprofessional on building root word models.

Base Words- stand-alone linguistic unit which cannot be deconstructed or broken down into smaller words. For example, in the word "re-tell," the base word is "tell."

Contractions- shortened forms of two words in which a letter or letters have been deleted. These deleted letters have been replaced by an apostrophe.

Prefixes- beginning units of meaning which can be added (the vocabulary word for this type of structural adding is "affixed") to a base word or root word. They can not stand alone. They are also sometimes known as "bound morphemes" meaning that they can not stand alone as a base word.

Suffixes- ending units of meaning which can be "affixed" or added on to the ends of root or base words. Suffixes transform the original meanings of base and root words. Like prefixes, they are also known as "bound morphemes," because they can not stand alone as words.

Compound Words- occur when two or more base words are connected to form a new word. The meaning of the new word is in some way connected with that of the base word.

Inflectional Endings- types of suffixes that impart a new meaning to the base or root word. These endings in particular change the gender, number, tense, or form of the base or root words. Just like other suffixes, these are also termed "bound morphemes."

Comments

Definitions are included because the structural analysis components are explicitly taught in schools which advocate the phonics-centered approach and are also incorporated into the word work component of the schools which advocate the balanced literacy approach for instruction.

Definition questions, that is multiple choice questions which have only a single right answer because they are testing whether the teacher candidate has memorized the appropriate content usage of the terms. They constitute for no less than 15% of the multiple choice question on the test. Therefore by taking the time to memorize these easy definitions scores are more likely to improve.

Knowledge of Greek and Latin Roots That Form English Words

Knowledge of Greek and Latin roots which comprise English words can measurably enhance children's reading skills and can also enrich their writing.

Word Webs

Sharon Taberski (2000) does not advocate teaching Greek and Latin derivatives in the abstract to young children. However, when she comes across (as is common and natural) specific Greek and Latin roots while reading to children, she uses that opportunity to introduce children to these rich resources.

For example, during readings on rodents (a favorite of first and second graders), Taberski draws her class's attention to the fact that beavers, gnaw at things with their teeth. She then connects the "dent" root or derivative to the children's lives, other words they are familiar with or experiences. The children then volunteer "*dentist," "dental," "denture."* Taberski begins to place these in a graphic organizer, or word web.

When she has tapped the extent of the children's prior knowledge of "dent" words, she shares with them the fact that *dens/dentis* is the Latin word for teeth. Then she introduces the word "indent," which she has already previewed with them as part of their conventions of print study. She helps them to see that the "indenting" of the first line of a paragraph can even be related to the "teeth" Latin root in that it looks like a "print" bite was taken out of the paragraph.

Taberski displays the word web in the Word Wall Chart section of her room. The class is encouraged throughout, say, a week's time to look for other words to add to the web. Taberski stresses that for her, as an elementary teacher of reading and writing, the key element of the Greek and Latin word root web activity is the children's coming to understand that if they know what a Greek or Latin word root means, they can use that knowledge to figure out what other words mean.

She feels the key concept is to model and demonstrate for children how fun and fascinating Greek and Latin root study can be.

Greek and Latin Roots Word Webs With an Assist From the World Wide Web

Older children in grades 3-6 can build on this initial print activity by searching online for additional words with a particular Greek or Latin root which has been introduced in class.

They can easily do this in a way that authentically ties in with their own interests and experiences by reading reviews for a book which has been a read-aloud online or by just reading the summaries of the day's news and printing out those words which appear in the stories online that share the root discussed.

The children can be encouraged to circle these instances of their Latin or Greek root and also to document the exact date and URL for the citation. These can be posted as part of their own online web in the word wall section study area. If the school or class has a website or webpage, the children can post this data there as a special Greek and Latin root word page.

Expanding the concept of the Greek and Latin word web from the printed page to the world wide web, nicely inculcates the child in the habits of lifelong reading and researching online. This beginning expository research will serve them well in intermediate level content area work and beyond.

Use of Syllabification as a Word Identification Strategy

Strategy: Clap Hands, Count those Syllables as They Come!! (Taberski, 2000)

The objective of this activity is for children to understand that there are every syllable in a polysyllabic word can be studied for its spelling patterns in the same way that monosyllabic words are studied for their spelling patterns.

The easiest way for the K-3 teacher to introduce this activity to the children is to share a familiar poem from the poetry chart (or to write out a familiar poem on a large experiential chart).

First the teacher reads the poem with the children. As they are reading it aloud, the children clap the beats of the poem and the teacher uses a colored marker to place a tic (/) above each syllable.

Next, the teacher takes letter cards and selects one of the polysyllabic words from the poem which the children have already "clapped" out.

The children use letter cards to spell that word on the sentence strip holder or it can be placed on a felt board or up against a window on display. Together the children and teacher divide the letters into syllables and place blank letter cards between the syllables. The children identify spelling patterns they know.

Finally and as part of continued small group syllabification study, the children identify other polysyllabic words they clapped out from the poem. They make up the letter combinations of these words. Then they separate them into syllables with blank letter cards between the syllables.

Children who require special support in syllabification can be encouraged to use many letter cards to create a large butcher paper syllabic (in letter cards with spaces) representation of the poem or at least a few lines of the poem. They can be told that this is for use as a teaching tool for others. In this way, they authenticate their study of syllabification with a real product that can actually be referenced by peers.

Techniques for Identifying Compound Words

The teaching of compound words should utilize structural analysis techniques. (See above section on structural analysis).
Here are some other strategies for helping students to identify and read compound words.

- Use songs and actions to help children understand the concept that compound words are two smaller words joined together to make one bigger word
- Use games like concentration, memory and go fish for students to practice reading compound words
- Use word sorts to have students distinguish between compound words and nonexamples of compound words

Identification of Homographs

Homographs are words that are spelled the same but have different meanings. A subgroup within this area includes words that are spelled the same, have different meanings, and are pronounced differently. Some examples of homographs include:

- Lie
- Tear
- Bow
- Fair
- Bass

Teaching homographs can be interesting and fun for the students. Incorporating them into passages where the students can use the context clues to decipher the different meanings of the homographs. Games are also a good strategy for using to help students understand multiple meaning words. Jokes and riddles are usually based on homographs, and students love to make collections or books of these.

Semantic Feature Analysis: This technique for enhancing vocabulary skills by using semantic cues is based on the research of Johnson and Pearson (1984) and Anders and Bos (1986). It involves young children in setting up a feature analysis grid of various subject content words which is an outgrowth of their discussion about these words.

For instance, Cooper (2004) includes a sample of a Semantic Features Analysis Grid for Vegetables. .

Vegetables	Green	Have Peels	Eat Raw	Seeds
Carrots	-	+	+	-
Cabbage	+	-	+	-

Note: that the use of the + for yes, - for no, and possible use for + and - if a vegetable like squash could be both green and yellow.

Teachers of children in grade one and beyond can design their own semantic analysis grids to meet their students' needs and to align with the topics the kids are learning. Select a category or class of words (could be planets, rodent family members, winter words, weather words).

Use the left side of the grid to list at least three if not more items that fit this category. The number of actual items listed will depend on the age and grade level of the children with three or four items fine for K-1 and up to 10-15 for grades 5 and 6. Brainstorm with the children or if better suited to the class, the teacher may list on his/her own features that the items have in common. As can be noted from the example excerpted from *Cooper's Literacy -Helping Children Construct Meaning* (2004), these common features such as vegetables' green color, peels, and seeds are usually fairly easy to identify.

Show the children how to insert the notations +, -, and even ?, (If they are not certain) on the grid. The teacher might also explore with the children the possibility that an item could get both a + and a -. For example, a vegetable like broccoli might be eaten cooked or raw depending on taste and squash can be green or yellow.

Whatever the length of the grid when first presented to the children (perhaps as a semantic cue lesson in and of itself tied in to a text being read in class), make certain that the grid as presented and filled out is not the end of the activity.

Children can use it as a model for developing their own semantic features grids and share them with the whole class. Child-developed grids can become part of a Word Work center in the classroom or even be published in a Word Study Games book by the class as a whole. Such a publication can be shared with parents during open school week and evening visits and with peer classes.

Contextual Redefinition

This strategy encourages children to use the context more effectively by presenting them with sufficient context BEFORE they begin reading. It models for the children the use of contextual clues to make informed guesses about word meanings.

To apply this strategy, the teacher should first select unfamiliar words for teaching. No more than two or three words should be selected for direct teaching. The teacher should then write a sentence in which there are sufficient clues supplied for the child to successfully figure out the meaning. Among the types of context clues the teacher can use are: compare/contrast, synonyms, and direct definition.

Then the teacher should present the words only on the experiential chart or as letter cards. Have the children pronounce the words. As they pronounce them, challenge them to come up with a definition for each word. After more than one definition is offered, encourage the children to decide as a whole group what the definition is. Write down their agreed upon definition with no comment as to its accurate meaning.

Then share with the children the contexts (sentences the teacher wrote with the words and explicit context clues). Ask that the children to read the sentences aloud. Then have them come up with a definition for each word. Make certain that as they present their definitions, the teacher does not comment. Ask that they justify their definitions by making specific references to the context clues in the sentences. As the discussion continues, direct the children's attention to their previously agreed upon definition of the word. Facilitate their discussing the differences between their guesses about the word when they saw only the word itself and their guesses about the word when they read it in context. Finally have the children check their use of context skills to correctly define the word by using a dictionary.

Teaching children ways to identify vowel-sound combinations and syllabic words

For children, the ability to identify vowel-sound combinations and syllabic words is contingent on familiarity of sounds that when combined can produce identifiable words. There are vowel sound essentials that create visual opportunities for children learning the phonics of vowel letter combinations. Children who are able to memorize all of the vowel sounds will learn how to spell and read faster according to researchers.

The vowel sound essentials include the following vowel letter combinations:

- Short vowels: a, e, i, o, and u
- Long vowels: a, e, i, o, and u
- Diagraphs (2 letters that produce 1 sound): ai, ee, ie, oa, ay, au, and aw
- Diphthongs (2 letters with 2 sounds): ou, oo-long/short, ew, ow-long/short, oi
- R vowels: ar, er, ir, or, ur

When children are encouraged to identify and memorize the basic vowel sound essentials, they are able to synthesize their learning into the decoding of new words and text. In most school communities, children are taught the memorization of basic consonants' sounds, but not the memorization of vowel sound essentials.

The application of vowel sounds to syllabic words creates an additional avenue of reading and word meaning support for children increasing reading ability and word usage. Children who have an understanding and memorization of the vowel sound essentials are able to increase their decoding strategy of new words by a higher percentage than children who base comprehension on predictable text of known words and usage.

In syllabic understanding, children are being asked to understand the organization of a sequence of speech sounds that formalize words. Syllables are word building blocks that provide pronunciation patterns and rhythm to language. Monosyllable words such as "cat or hat" consist of speech patterns that use consonants and vowels to form a singular sound. As words become more complex in syllabic construct, they can consist of two syllables, disyllable (reader) up to more than four syllables, polysyllable (i.e. communication).

The phonetics of syllabic words includes a core nucleus of vowel sounds that can be viewed in common words as a "consonant-vowel-consonant" sequence of letters and sounds. Longer syllabic words such as "imagination" have stress and tone on each part of the syllabic segments that includes a phonetic emphasis on the core nucleus of the word. Children learning to understand the contextual meaning of words must understand the vowel and syllabic construction to word formation and usage.

Skill 10.2 Demonstrate knowledge of techniques for decoding text using context clues

To decode means to change communication signals into messages. Reading comprehension requires that the reader learn the code within which a message is written and be able to decode it to get the message.

Although effective reading comprehension requires identifying words automatically (Adams, 1990, Perfetti, 1985), children do not have to be able to identify every single word or know the exact meaning of the every word in a text to understand it. Indeed, Nagy (1988) says that, children can read a work with a high level of comprehension even if they do not fully know as many as 15 percent of the words within a given text.

Children develop the ability to decode and recognize words automatically. They then can extend their ability to decode to multi-syllabic words.
J. David Cooper (2004) and other advocates of the Balanced Literacy Approach, feel that children become literate, effective communicators and able to comprehend, by learning phonics and other aspects of word identification through the use of engaging reading texts. Engaging text, as defined by the balanced literacy group, are those texts which contain highly predictable elements of rhyme, sound patterns, and plot. Researchers, such as Chall (1983) and Flesch (1981), support a phonics-centered foundation before the use of engaging reading texts. This is at the crux of the phonics versus whole language/ balanced literacy/ integrated language arts, teaching of reading controversy.

It is important for the new teacher to be informed about both sides of this controversy, as well as the work of theorists who attempt to reconcile these two perspectives, such as Kenneth Goodman (1994). There are powerful arguments on both sides of this controversy, and each approach works wonderfully with some students and does not succeed with others.

As far as the examinations go, all that is asked of you is the ability to demonstrate that you are familiar with these varied perspectives. If asked on a constructed response question, you need to be able to show that you can talk about teaching some aspect of reading using strategies from one or the other or a combination of both approaches.

This guide is designed to provide you with numerous strategies representing both approaches.

The working teacher can, depending on the perspective of his /her school administration and the needs of the particular children he or she serves, choose from the strategies and approaches which work best for the children concerned.

Blending Letter Sounds

Prompts for Graphophonic Cues

You said (the child's incorrect attempt). Does that match the letters you see?
If it were the word you just said, (the child's incorrect attempt), what would it have to start with?

If it were the word you just said (the child's incorrect attempt), what would it have to end with?

Look at the first letter/s . . . look at the middle letter/s
. . . the last letter. . What could it be?

If you were writing (the child's incorrect attempt) what letter would you write first?
What letters would go in the middle?
What letters would go last?

A good strategy to use in working with individual children is to have them explain how they finally correctly identified a word that was troubling them. If prompted and habituated through one on one teacher/tutoring conversations, they can be quite clear about what they did to "get" the word.

If the children are already writing their own stories, the teacher might say to them: "You know when you write your own stories, you would never write any story which did not make sense. You wouldn't and probably this writer didn't either. If you read something that does make sense, but doesn't match the letters, then it's probably not what the author wrote. This is the author's story, not yours right now, so go back to the word and see if you can find out the author's story. Later on, you might write your own story."

Letter Sound Correspondence and Beginning Decoding

Use this procedure for letter-sound investigations that support beginning decoding. First, focus on a particular letter/s which you want the child to investigate. It is good to choose one from a shared text which the children are familiar with. Make certain that the teachers' directions to the children are clear and either focuses them on looking for a specific letter or listening for sounds.

Next, begin a list of words that meet the task given to the children. Use chart paper to list the words that the children identify. This list can be continued into the next week as long as the children's focus is maintained on the list. This can be easily done by challenging the children with identifying a specific number of letters or sounds and "daring" them as a class team to go beyond those words or sounds.

Third, continue to add to the list. Focus the children at the beginning of the day on the goal of their individually adding to the list. Give them an adhesive note (sticky pad sheet) on which they can individually write down the words they find. Then they can attach their newly found words with their names on them to the chart. This provides the children with a sense of ownership and pride in their letter-sounding abilities. During shared reading, discuss the children's proposed additions and have the group decide if these meet the directed category. If all the children agree that they do meet the category, include the words on the chart.

Fourth, do a word sort from all the words generated and have the children put the words into categories that demonstrate similarities and differences. They can be prompted to see if the letter appeared at the beginning of the word, or in the end of the word. They might also be prompted to see that one sound could have two different letter representations. The children can then "box" the word differences and similarities by drawing colors established in a chart key.

Finally, before the children go off to read, ask them to look for new words in the texts which they can now recognize because of the letter sound relationships on their chart. During shared reading, make certain that they have time to share these words they were able to decode because of their explorations.

Strategies for Helping Students Decode Single Syllable Words that Follow Common Patterns and Multi-syllable Words

(This activity is presented in detail so it can actually be implemented with children in an intermediate classroom and also to provide detail for a potential constructed response question on a certification examination.)

The CVC phonics card game developed by Jackie Montierth, a computer teacher in South San Diego for use with 5th and 6th grade students, is a good one to adapt to the needs of any group with appropriate modifications for age, grade level and language needs.

The children use the vehicle of the card game to practice and enhance their use of consonants and vowels. Their fluency in this will increase their ability to decode words. Potential uses beyond whole classroom instruction include use as part of the small group word work component of the reading workshop and as part of cooperative team learning. This particular strategy also is particularly helpful for grade four and beyond English Language learners who are in a regular English Language classroom setting.

The card game works well because the practice of the content is implicit for transfer as the children continue to improve their reading skills. In addition, the card game format allows "instructional punctuation" using a student centered high interest exploration.

Card Design: The teacher can use the computer or use 5"x 8" index cards or actual card deck sized oaktag cards to create a deck. For repeated use and durability, it is recommended that the deck be laminated.

The deck should consist of the following:
44 consonant cards (including the blends)
15 vowel cards (including 3 of each vowel)
5 wild cards (which can be used as any vowel)
6 final e cards

The design of this project can also focus on particular CVC words that are part of a particular book, topic or genre format. In advance of playing the game, children can also be directed to review the words on the word wall or other words on a word map.

Procedure:

The game is best introduced first as part of a mini lesson with the teacher reading the rules, and a pair of children demonstrating step by step, when the game is played before the class for the first time. Have the children divide into pairs or small groups of no more than 4 per group. Each group needs one deck of C-V-C cards.

Have each group choose a dealer. The dealer shuffles the cards and deals 5 cards to each player. The remaining cards are placed face down for drawing during the play. One card is turned over to form the discard pile. Players may not show their cards to the other players. The first player to the left of the dealer looks at his/her cards and if possible, puts down three cards which make a consonant-vowel-consonant word. For more points, four cards forming a consonant-vowel-consonant word can be placed down. The player must then say the word and draw the number of cards he or she laid down. If he or she is unable to form a word, he/she draws either a card from either the draw or discard pile. The player then discards one card. All players must have 5 cards at all times. Play moves to the left.

The game continues until one or more of the following happens:
1. There are no more cards in the draw pile
2. All players run out of cards.
3. All players cannot form a word

The winner is the player who has laid down the most cards during the game.

Players may only lay down words at the beginning of their turn.
Proper names may not be counted as words.

Other ways the game may be played:

The game can be played with teams of individuals in a small group of four or fewer competing against one another (Excellent for special needs or resource room students). It can also be done as a whole class activity where all the students are divided into cooperative teams or small groups who compete against one another. This second approach will work well with a heterogeneous classroom that includes special needs and/or ELL children.

Teachers of ELL learners can do this game in the native language first and then transition it into English, facilitating native language reading skills and second language acquisition. They can develop their own appropriate decks to meet the vocabulary needs of their children and to complement the curricula.

Using Phonics to Decode Words in Connected Text

Identifying New Words

Some strategies to share with children during conferences or as part of shared reading include the following prompts:

- Look at the beginning letter/s... What sound do you hear?

- Stop to think about the text or story. What word with this beginning letter would make sense here?

- Look at the book's illustrations. Do they provide you with help in figuring out the new word?

- Think of what word would make sense, sound right, and match the letters that you see. Start the sentence over, making your mouth ready to say that word.

- Skip the word, read to the end of the sentence, and then come back to the word. How does what you've read help you with the word?

- Listen to whether what you are reading makes sense and matches the letters (asking the child to self-monitor). If it doesn't make sense, see if you can correct it on your own.

- Look for spelling patterns you know from the spelling pattern wall.

- Look for smaller words you might know within the larger word.

- Read on a little, and then return to the part that confused you.

Use of Semantic and Syntactic Cues to Help Decode Words

Semantic Cues

Students will need use their base knowledge of word meanings, semantics, to help them decipher unknown words or text as well as to clarify reading when it does not seem to make sense. Some prompts the teacher can use which will alert the children to semantic cues include:
- Does that sentence make sense?
- Which word in that sentence does not seem to fit?
- Why doesn't it fit?
- What word might make sense in that sentence?

Syntactic Cues

The first strategy good readers use from their own knowledge base to help determine misreading, is syntactic cues. Syntactic cues use the order of words and the student's knowledge of the oral English language to help determine if what was read could be accurate. Some prompts the teacher can use to encourage and develop syntactic cues in reading include:
- You read (child's incorrect attempt). Does that sound right?
- You read (child's incorrect attempt). When we talk, do we talk that way?
- How would we say it?
- Recheck that sentence. Does it sound right the way you read it?

Specific Terminology Associated With Phonics

It is important to have a clear understanding of the terms associated with phonics. Here are some definitions, which are helpful in having a clear understanding of phonic development in children.

Phoneme – a phoneme is the smallest unit of sound in the English language. In print phonemes are represented by the letter and a slash. So, /b/ represents the sound the letter b would make.

Morpheme- a morpheme is the smallest unit of grammar in the English language. In other words, it is the smallest unit of meaning, not just sounds.

Consonant Digraph – a consonant digraph are two consonants of the English language who when placed together in a word make a unique sound, neither makes when alone. Examples: ch, th, sh, and wh.

Consonant Blend- a consonant blend is when two consonants are put together, but each retains their individual sound. The two sounds go together in a seamless manner to produce a blended sound. Examples: st, br, cl, etc.

Schwa sound- schwa sound is a vowel sound which is neutral. It typically occurs in the unaccented syllable of a word. An example would be the sound of the a at the end of the word sofa. It is represented in print by an upside down e

It is inevitable in reading that students will come across words they are unable to read. When this happens, the student will need to a variety of strategies to draw upon to not only figure out the unknown word, but to also be able to gather meaning from the word and text.

Students typically begin with decoding, or the application of phonics skills, when they come across an unknown word. If they are unable to correctly decode the word, they may use some other strategies including structural analysis and context clues.

In structural analysis, the student uses word patterns and parts they recognize to help them figure out unknown words. In this way, students are looking at larger portions of word parts rather than with decoding where they may be looking at no more than two letters together.

Contextual reading is something we all do from a very young age to adult years. Sometimes regardless the ability to decode or apply structural analysis, there are words we are still unable to read. In this case, the reader can use other words in the sentence or paragraph to help decide the unknown word.

Good readers use the syntax, or the manner in which the sentence is put together, to help determine meaning from context. They also find ways to put the sentence or passage in their own words or look for contrasting ideas. All of these strategies help the reader to draw meaning from what is being read. This frame of reference helps to provide more details for the reader. Contrast is also a method readers may use to build context or determine meaning.

All of these strategies together help readers develop comprehension when reading. However, sometimes words have more than one meaning. In this case, the student may be able to identify the word, but still have difficulty determining meaning. In some cases, meaning can be confusing as the student only knows one meaning of the word, and when reading, it simply does not make sense. It is in this instance that the use of context clues can be most beneficial. Students can begin to learn more than one meaning by basing their analysis on the rest of the words in the passage. In this way, they can learn the multiple meanings of words without having to rely on skill and drill vocabulary activities.

Teaching children to read passages using decodable texts

Teachers can provides a multitude of opportunities for children to progress from sounding out words orally to decoding words silently. When a child decodes a text that is age appropriate, he or she is able to look at the spelling and pronunciation of specific words that are familiar. The Cat in the Hat book series provides children with story scenarios that are rhythmic and patterned. Crucial to decoding is the child's knowledge of word meaning from a prior knowledge and current word usage.

Decoding text is age appropriate for children who have existing knowledge of the reading material. When children decode words they are able to read single words and understand meaning of single words as singular entities in a textual context. There is a foundational pattern to language acquisition that children must first develop before the complexity of decoding text can begin. Children must be able to learn individual alphabet sounds and understand that each letter has a sound. As students progress from alphabet sound, they can learn about how letters are put together to form words that produce different sounds and meanings.

As children gather a phonemic awareness of word sounds, their ability to read words in text and acquire meaning for what they are reading creates a framework for sound-letter connection. It is during this discovery of phonemic sounds of word patterns that enables students to develop effective reading patterns. Providing opportunities for children to sound out words using software programs that use microphones to encourage students to practice word sounds can become powerful tools as children acquire language and word development. Visual tutorials with adult instruction create another effective opportunity for children to work on decoding skills and get instant feedback from a knowledgeable instructor.

Classroom and social interactions that create child-centered opportunities to question, respond and decode the world around them can create bridges of understanding in decoding simple and complex words and language into smaller understandable chunks of relevant information. Providing children with lessons and activities that require decoding to understand a context of meaning will provide practice for decoding mechanics. For example children who are engaged in a dramatic play must understand the simple phrases that constitute meaning for the parts they portray. Having that incentive to use decoding skills will promote the acquisition of language development.

Teaching children to recognize high-frequency irregular words

A child's ability to recognize high-frequency irregular words through a selection process of choosing words in regular children's books and reviewing difficult words frequently can provide a comprehensive vocabulary listing. When children learn the decoding of regular words in children's books, the foundational learning of decoding strategies can help children recognize and provide phonetic pronunciation to new words.

Word acquisition for children is directly correlated with environmental stimuli, adult engagement in learning and normal speech and language development. When children at 18-23 months are able to understand functional words that occur in their daily lives such as "eat, sleep, talk, ear nose, mouth," they have begun the ability to associate words with activities or body parts. As children learn how to pronounce words that contain vowels and begin with soft consonants such as n, m, h, speech development occurs.

The clarity of speech during the younger years is more like sound mimics as children review simple words such as "milk or moo." Children who are between the ages of 3-4 have on average 50 words that can be simulated in book reading to differentiate regular word usage from the introduction of irregular words in their vocabulary. During this age range children can be introduced to a diversity of high frequency irregular words that are used intermittently in books and reading resources.

By the age of five years old, children have acquired a database of about 2,000 words and a multitude of expression formations that include the ability to learn irregular words and understand their contextual cues and applications in story formations. Providing children with constant review of new words can create a constant stream of language acquisition for young minds that act as sponges soaking up the presents of words, experiences, and opportunities of speech and language application.

When high frequency irregular words are isolated from the contextual resources and presented to children as activities that require definition, pronunciation, application, and synthesis, children are able to master and internalize the words more thoroughly. Classroom and learning opportunities to have exposure to irregular words are beneficial for children seeking to increase reading, vocabulary and communication skills.

Language and oral development are contingent upon children being provided with a diversity of word applications for use in language development and oral communication. As more irregular words are constantly being added to the Webster Dictionary, a child's vocabulary list is becoming inclusive of irregular words that are now becoming today's regular words in communication and written application.

Skill 10.3   Demonstrate knowledge of prereading strategies for students (e.g., skimming, making predictions)

Throughout their lives students will be reading for a variety of purposes and a multitude of different texts. The purpose behind reading often drives the type of reading completed by the student. The type of text can also drive the type of reading strategies the students use to successfully navigate the information. When reading for pleasure, students tend to read less carefully and they may even skim some portions of the text. As the book is simply for pleasure, this is perfectly acceptable and should be allowed. In fact, skimming skills can be introduced and used for other types of readings. Students who are looking for vocabulary words or definitions may skim a great deal of information at a more rapid pace before finding the appropriate part of the passage. This is also a good strategy when used to find any specific pieces of information.

In addition to skimming, scanning is another technique students can use to look through a large amount of text for specific details and/or information. This can be particularly helpful in searching through different books to determine if any of the information is pertinent to meet the needs of the student.

Teachers need to take the time to teach students when it is necessary to reread information. Typically, students understand that it is important to reread when something is not understood clearly. However, there are other times when rereading may be important. In content-heavy texts, rereading can not only provide further clarification, but it can also provide additional details the reader may have missed the first time. It is easy to miss information when so much is packed into small passages. Thus, rereading can be an important factor in learning and making sure they have taken in all of the details.

In-depth reading can be a fatiguing task and cannot be completed on all books students will encounter. Reading with the specific eye for details, students need to understand this process and that it is called for mostly in nonfiction texts which are laden with information. When reading in depth, students are trying to intake as much information as possible. It requires concentration and a concerted effort.

The point of comprehension instruction is not necessarily to focus just on the text(s) students are using at the very moment of instruction, but rather to help them learn the strategies that they can use independently with any other text. Some of the most common methods of teaching instruction are as follows:

- Summarization: This is where, either in writing or verbally, students go over the main point of the text, along with strategically chosen details that highlight the main point. This is not the same as paraphrasing, which is saying the same thing in different words. Teaching students how to summarize is very important as it will help them look for the most critical areas in a text, and in non-fiction. For example, it will help them distinguish between main arguments and examples. In fiction, it helps students to learn how to focus on the main characters and events and distinguish those from the lesser characters and events.

- Question answering: While this tends to be over-used in many classrooms, it is still a valid method of teaching students to comprehend. As the name implies, students answer questions regarding a text, either out loud, in small groups, or individually on paper. The best questions are those that cause students to have to think about the text (rather than just find an answer within the text).

- Question generating: This is the opposite of question answering, although students can then be asked to answer their own questions or the questions of peer students. In general, we want students to constantly question texts as they read. This is important because it causes students to become more critical readers. To teach students to generate questions helps them to learn the types of questions they can ask, and it gets them thinking about how best to be critical of texts.

- Graphic organizers: Graphic organizers are graphical representations of content within a text. For example, Venn Diagrams can be used to highlight the difference between two characters in a novel or two similar political concepts in a Social Studies textbook. Or, a teacher can use flow-charts with students to talk about the steps in a process (for example, the steps of setting up a science experiment or the chronological events of a story). Semantic organizers are similar in that they graphically display information. The difference, usually, is that semantic organizers focus on words or concepts. For example, a word web can help students make sense of a word by mapping from the central word all the similar and related concepts to that word.

- Text structure: Often in non-fiction, particularly in textbooks, and sometimes in fiction, text structures will give important clues to readers about what to look for. Often, students do not know how to make sense of all the types of headings in a textbook and do not realize that, for example, the side-bar story about a character in history is not the main text on a particular page in the history textbook. Teaching students how to interpret text structures gives them tools in which to tackle other similar texts.

- Monitoring comprehension: Students need to be aware of their comprehension, or lack of it, in particular texts. So, it is important to teach students what to do when suddenly text stops making sense. For example, students can go back and re-read the description of a character. Or, they can go back to the table of contents or the first paragraph of a chapter to see where they are headed.

- Textual marking: This is where students interact with the text as they read. For example, armed with Post-it Notes, students can insert questions or comments regarding specific sentences or paragraphs within the text. This helps students focus on the importance of the small things, particularly when they are reading larger works (such as novels in high school). It also gives students a reference point on which to go back into the text when they need to review something.

- Discussion: Small group or whole-class discussion stimulates thoughts about texts and gives students a larger picture of the impact of those texts. For example, teachers can strategically encourage students to discuss related concepts to the text. This helps students learn to consider texts within larger societal and social concepts, or teachers can encourage students to provide personal opinions in discussion. By listening to various students' opinions, this will help all students in a class to see the wide range of possible interpretations and thoughts regarding one text.

Many people mistakenly believe that the terms "research-based" or "research-validated" or "evidence-based" relate mainly to specific programs, such as early reading textbook programs. While research does validate that some of these programs are effective, much research has been conducted regarding the effectiveness of particular instructional strategies. In reading, many of these strategies have been documented in the report from the National Reading Panel (2000). However, just because a strategy has not been validated as effective by research does not necessarily mean that it is not effective with certain students in certain situations. The number of strategies out there far outweighs researchers' ability to test their effectiveness. Some of the strategies listed above have been validated by rigorous research, while others have been shown consistently to help improve students' reading abilities in localized situations. There simply is not enough space to list all the strategies out there that have been proven effective; just know that the above strategies are very commonly cited ones that work in a variety of situations.

Skill 10.4   Demonstrate knowledge of methods for determining how well students are comprehending what they read

Students need to be aware of their comprehension, or lack of it, in particular texts. So, it is important to teach students what to do when suddenly text stops making sense. For example, students can go back and re-read the description of a character. Or, they can go back to the table of contents or the first paragraph of a chapter to see where they are headed

Comprehension simply means that the reader can ascribe meaning to text. Even though students may be good with phonics and even know what many words on a page mean, some of them are not good with comprehension because they do not know the strategies that would help them to comprehend. For example, students should know that stories often have structures (beginning, middle, and end). They should also know that when they are reading something and it does not make sense, they will need to employ "fix-up" strategies where they go back into the text they just read and look for clues. Teachers can use many strategies to teach comprehension, including questioning, asking students to paraphrase or summarize, utilizing graphic organizers, and focusing on mental images.

The point of comprehension instruction is not necessarily to focus just on the text(s) students are using at the very moment of instruction, but rather to help them learn the strategies that they can use independently with any other text. Some of the most common methods of teaching instruction are listed here:

Making Predictions

One theory or approach to the teaching of reading that gained currency in the late sixties and the early seventies was the importance of asking inferential and critical thinking questions of the reader which would challenge and engage the children in the text. This approach to reading went beyond the literal level of what was stated in the text to an inferential level of using text clues to make predictions and to a critical level of involving the child in evaluating the text. While asking engaging and thought-provoking questions is still viewed as part of the teaching of reading, it is only viewed currently as a component of the teaching of reading.

Prior Knowledge

Prior knowledge can be defined as all of an individual's prior experiences, learning, and development which precede his/her entering a specific learning situation or attempting to comprehend a specific text. Sometimes prior knowledge can be erroneous or incomplete. Obviously, if there are misconceptions in a child's prior knowledge, these must be corrected so that the child's overall comprehension skills can continue to progress. Prior knowledge, of even kindergarteners includes their accumulated positive and negative experiences both in and out of school.

These might range from wonderful family travels, watching television, visiting museums and libraries, to visiting hospitals, prisons and surviving poverty. Whatever the prior knowledge that the child brings to the school setting, the independent reading and writing the child does in school immeasurably expands his/her prior knowledge and hence broadens his/her reading comprehension capabilities. Literary response skills are dependent on prior knowledge, schemata and background. Schemata (the plural of schema) are those structures which represent generic concepts stored in our memory. Effective comprehenders of text, whether they are adults or children, use both their schemata and prior knowledge PLUS the ideas from the printed text for reading comprehension, and graphic organizers help organize this information.

Graphic Organizers

Graphic organizers solidify in a chart format a visual relationship among various reading and writing ideas including: sequence, timelines, character traits, fact and opinion, main idea and details, differences and likenesses (generally done using a VENN DIAGRAM of interlocking circles, KWL Chart, etc). These charts and formats are essential for providing scaffolding for instruction through activating pertinent prior knowledge.

KWL charts are exceptionally useful for reading comprehension by outline what they KNOW, what they WANT to know, and what they've LEARNED after reading. Students are asked to activate prior knowledge about a topic and further develop their knowledge about a topic using this organizer. Teachers often opt to display and maintain KWL charts throughout a text to continually record pertinent information about students' reading.

When the teacher first introduces the K-W-L strategy, the children should be allowed sufficient time to brainstorm in response to the first question, what all of them in the class or small group actually know about the topic. The children should have a three-columned K-W-L worksheet template for their journals and there should be a chart to record the responses from class or group discussion. The children can write under each column in their own journal, and should also help the teacher educator with notations on the chart. This strategy involves the children actually gaining experience in note taking and having a concrete record of new data and information they have gleaned from the passage about the topic.

Depending on the grade level of the participating children, the teacher may also want to channel them into considering categories of information they hope to find out from the expository passage. For instance, they may be reading a book on animals to find out more about the animal's habitats during the winter or about the animal's mating habits.

When children are working on the middle-What I want to know section of their K-W-L strategy sheet, the teacher may want to give them a chance to share what they would like to learn further about the topic and help them to express it in question format.

K-W-L is useful and can even be introduced as early as grade two with extensive teacher discussion support. It not only serves to support the child's comprehension of a particular expository text, but also models for children a format for note taking. Beyond note taking, when the teacher wants to introduce report writing, the K-W-L format provides excellent outlines and question introductions for at least three paragraphs of a report.

Cooper (2004) recommends this strategy for use with thematic units and with reading chapters in required science, social studies, or health text books. In addition to its usefulness with thematic unit study, K-W-L is wonderful for providing the teacher with a concrete format to assess how well children have absorbed pertinent new knowledge within the passage (by looking at the third L section). Ultimately it is hoped that students will learn to use this strategy, not only under explicit teacher direction with templates of K-W-L sheets, but also on their own by informally writing questions they want to find out about in their journals and then going back to their own questions and answering them after the reading.

Retelling

Retelling needs to be very clearly defined so that the child reader does not think that the teacher wants him or her to spill the WHOLE story back in the retelling. A child should be able to talk comfortably and fluently about the story he or she has just read. He or she should be able to tell the main things that have happened in the story.

When a child retells a story to a teacher, the teacher needs ways to help him or her assess the child's understanding. Ironically, the teacher can use some of the same strategies he or she suggests to the child, to assess the child's understanding of a book which is not familiar to the teacher. These strategies include: back cover reading, scanning the table of contents, looking at the pictures, and reading the book jacket.

If the child can explain how the story turned out and provide examples to support these explanations, try not to interrupt him or her with too many questions.

Children can use the text of the book to reinforce what they are saying and they can even read from it if they wish. It is also important to note that some children need to re-read the text twice and their re-reading of it is out of enjoyment.

When the teacher plans to use the retelling as a way of assessing the child, then the following ground rules have to be set and made clear to the child.

The teacher explains the purpose of the retelling to determine how well the child is reading at the outset of the conference.

The teacher maintains in the child's assessment notebook or in his/her assessment record for him what the child is saying in phrases, not sentences. Just enough is recorded to indicate whether the child actually understood the story. The teacher also tries to analyze from the retelling why the child can not comprehend a given text. If the child's accuracy rate with the text is below 95 per cent, then the problem is at the word level, but the accuracy rate for the text is above 95 per cent, the difficulty lies at the text level.

Inferencing

Inferencing is an evaluative process that involves the reader making a reasonable judgment based on the information given and engages children in literally constructing meaning. In order to develop and enhance this key skill in children, they might have a mini lesson where the teacher demonstrates this key skill by reading an expository book aloud (i.e. one on skyscrapers for young children) and then demonstrates for them the following reading habits: looking for clues, reflecting on what the reader already knows about the topic ("activating prior knowledge in a teacher's jargon), and using the clues in the expository text to figure out what the author means/intends.

Main Idea

Identifying main ideas in an expository text can be improved when the children have an explicit strategy for identifying important information. They can be include into making this strategy part of their everyday reading style, by being focused and "walked" through the following exercises as apart of a series of guided reading sessions. The child should read the passage so that the topic is readily identifiable to him or her. It will be what most of the information is about.

Next the child should be asked to be on the lookout for a sentence within the expository passage that summarizes the key information in the paragraph or in the lengthier excerpt. Then the child should read the rest of the passage or excerpt in light of this information and also note which information in the paragraph is not important. The important information the child has identified in the paragraph can be used by the child reader to formulate the author's main idea. The child reader may even want to use some of the author's own language in formulating that idea.

Monitoring

Monitoring means self-clarifying: As a reader reads, the reader often realizes that what he or she is reading is not making sense. The reader then has to have a plan for making sensible meaning out of the excerpt. Cooper and other balanced literacy advocates have a stop and think strategy which they use with children. The child reflects, "Does this make sense to me?" When the child concludes that it does not, the child then either: re-reads, reads ahead in the text, looks up unknown words or asks for help from the teacher.

What is important about monitoring is that some readers ask these questions and try these approaches without ever being explicitly taught them in school by a teacher. However, the key philosophy of the foundations of reading theorists mentioned here is that these strategies need to be explicitly modeled and practiced under the guidance of the teacher by most, if not all child readers.

Summarizing

Summarizing engages the reader in pulling together into a cohesive whole, the essential bits of information within a longer passage or excerpt of text. Children can be taught to summarize informational or expository text by following these guidelines. First they should look at the topic sentence of the paragraph or the text and delete the trivia. Then they should search for information which has been mentioned more than once and make sure it is included only once in their summary. Then find related ideas or items and group them under a unifying heading. Search for and identify a main idea sentence. Put the summary together using all these guidelines.

Discussing the Text

Discussion is an activity in which the children (and this activity works well from grades 3-6 and beyond) conclude a particular text. Among the prompts, the teacher-coach might suggest that the children focus on words of interest they encountered in the text. These can also be words that they heard if the text was read aloud. Children can be asked to share something funny or upsetting or unusual about the words they have read. Through this focus on children's response to words as the center of the discussion circle, peers become more interested in word study.

Furthermore, in the current teaching of literacy, reading, writing, thinking, listening, viewing, and discussing, are not viewed as separate activities or components of instruction, but rather as developing and being nurtured simultaneously and interactively.

Teachers should have a toolkit of instructional strategies, materials and technologies to encourage and teach students how to problem solve and think critically about subject content. With each curriculum chosen by a district for school implementation, comes an expectation that students must master benchmarks and standards of learning skills. There is an established level of academic performance and proficiency in public schools that students are required to master in today's classrooms. Research of national and state standards indicate that there additional benchmarks and learning objectives in the subject areas of science, foreign language, English language arts, history, art, health, civics, economics, geography, physical education, mathematics, and social studies that students are required to master in state assessments (Marzano & Kendall, 1996).

A critical thinking skill is a skill target that teachers help students develop to sustain learning in specific subject areas that can be applied within other subject areas. For example, when learning to understand algebraic concepts in solving a math word problem on how much fencing material is needed to build a fence around a backyard area that has a 8' x 12," a math student must understand the order of numerical expression in how to simplify algebraic expressions. Teachers can provide instructional strategies that show students how to group the fencing measurements into an algebraic word problem that with minor addition, subtraction and multiplication can produce a simple number equal to the amount of fencing materials needed to build the fence.

Higher-Ordered Thinking Skills

Developing critical thinking skills in students is not as simple as developing other simpler skills. In fact, many teachers mistakenly believe that these skills can be taught out of context (i.e., they can be taught as skills in and of themselves). Good teachers, however, realize that critical thinking skills must be taught within the contexts of specific subject matter. For example, language arts teachers can teach critical thinking skills through novels; social studies teachers can teach critical thinking skills through primary source documents or current events; science teachers can teach critical thinking skills by having students develop hypotheses prior to conducting experiments.

First, let's start with definitions of the various types of critical thinking skills. Analysis is the systematic exploration of a concept, event, term, piece of writing, element of media, or any other complex item. Usually, people think of analysis as the exploration of the parts that make up a whole. For example, when someone analyzes a piece of literature, that person might focus on small pieces of the literature; yet, as they focus on the small pieces, they also call attention to the big picture and show how the small pieces create significance for the whole novel.

To carry this example further, if one were to analyze a novel, that person might investigate a particular character to determine how that character adds significance to the whole novel. In something more concrete like biology, one could analyze the findings of an experiment to see if the results might indicate significance for something even larger than the experiment itself. It is very easy to analyze political events, for example. A social studies teacher could ask students to analyze the events leading up to World War II: doing so would require that students look at the small pieces (e.g., smaller world events prior to World War II) and determine how those small pieces, when added up together, caused the war.

Next, let's consider synthesis. Synthesis is usually thought of to be the opposite of analysis. In analysis, we take a whole and break it up into pieces and look at the pieces. With synthesis, we take different things and make them one whole thing. For example, a language arts teacher could ask students to synthesize two works of distinct literature. Let's say that we take *The Scarlett Letter* and *The Crucible*, two works both featuring life during Puritanical America, written about one century apart. A student could synthesize the two works and come to conclusions about Puritanical life. An Art teacher could ask students to synthesize two paintings from the Impressionist era and come to conclusions about the features that distinguish that style of art.

Finally, evaluation involves making judgments. Whereas analysis and synthesis seek answers and hypotheses based on investigations, evaluation seeks opinions. For example, a social studies teacher could ask students to evaluate the quality of Richard Nixon's resignation speech. To do so, they would judge whether or not they felt it was good (according to some set of standards). In contrast, analysis would keep judgment out of the assignment: it would have students focus possibly on the structure of the speech (i.e., Does an argument move from emotional to logical?). When evaluating a speech, a piece of literature, a movie, or a work of art, we seek to determine whether one thinks it is good or not. But, keep in mind, teaching good evaluation skills requires not just that students learn how to determine whether something is good or not—it requires that they learn how to support their evaluations. So, if a student claims that Nixon's speech was effective in what the President intended the speech to do, the student would need to explain how this is so. Notice that evaluation will probably utilize the skills of analysis and/or synthesis, but that the purpose is ultimately different.

Encouraging Independent Critical Thinking

Since most teachers want their educational objectives to use higher level thinking skills, teachers need to direct students to these higher levels on the taxonomy. Questioning is an effective tool to build up students to these higher levels. Low order questions are useful to begin the process. They insure the student is focused on the required information and understands what needs to be included in the thinking process. For example, if the objective is for students to be able to read and understand the story "Goldilocks and the Three Bears," the teacher may wish to start with low order questions (i.e., "What are some things Goldilocks did while in the bears home?" [Knowledge] or "Why didn't Goldilocks like the Papa Bear's chair?" [Analysis]).

Through a series of questions, the teacher can move the students up the taxonomy. (For example, "If Goldilocks had come to your house, what are some things she may have used?" [Application], "How might the story differed if Goldilocks had visited the three fishes?" [Synthesis], or "Do you think Goldilocks was good or bad? Why?" [Evaluation]). The teacher through questioning can control the thinking process of the class. As students become more involved in the discussion they are systematically being lead to higher level thinking.

To develop a critical-thinking approach to the world, children need to know enough about valid and invalid reasoning to ask questions. Bringing into the classroom speeches or essays that demonstrate both valid and invalid examples can be useful in helping students develop the ability to question the reasoning of others. These will be published writers or televised speakers, so they can see that they are able even to question ideas that are accepted by some adults and talk about what is wrong in the thinking of those apparently successful communicators.

If the teacher stays right on the cutting edge of children's experience, they will become more and more curious about what is out there in the world that they don't know about. A lesson on a particular country or even a tribe in the world that the children may not even know exists that will use various kinds of media to reveal to them what life is like there for children their own age is a good way to introduce the world out there. In such a presentation, positive aspects of the lives of those "other" children should be included. Perhaps a correspondence with a village could be developed. It's good for children, some of whom may not live very high on the social scale in this country, to know what the rest of the world is like, and in so doing, develop an independent curiosity to know more.

In general, critical thinking skills should be taught through assignments, activities, lessons, and discussions that cause students to think on their own. While teachers can and should provide students with the tools to think critically, they will ultimately become critical thinkers if they have to use those tools themselves. But, this one last point cannot be taken lightly: Teachers must provide students the tools to evaluate, analyze, and synthesize.

Let's take political speeches as an example. Students will be better analyzers, synthesizers, and evaluators if they understand some of the basics of political speeches. Therefore, a teacher might introduce concepts such as rhetoric, style, persona, audience, diction, imagery, and tone. The best way to introduce these concepts would be to provide students with multiple, good examples of these things. Once they are familiar with these critical tools, students will be in a better place to apply them individually to political speeches—and then be able to analyze, synthesize, and evaluate political speeches on their own.

Skill 10.5 Demonstrate knowledge of methods for helping students interpret written directions

How does one get from here to there, from kindergarten to graduate school or to a trade school? The answer of course is by one step at a time, by carefully organizing one's courses of action, each phase building on the previous step and leading to the next.

Similarly, when taking a test you are asked to follow written instructions or directions the examiner wants to see how you manage your answer to the exam question. How do you organize your answer logically? How do you support your conclusions? How well connected are your ideas and the support you bring to your argument?

Look at how the writer does these tasks in the following essay:

Parenting Classes

Someone once said that the two most difficult jobs in the world - voting and being a parent - are given to rank amateurs. The consequences of this inequity are voter apathy and inept parenting leading to, on the one hand, an apparent failure of the democratic process and, on the other hand, misbehaving and misguided children.

The antidote for the first problem is in place in most school systems. Classes in history, civics, history, government, and student government provide a kind of "hands on" training in becoming an active member of society so that the step from student hood to citizenship is clear and expected.

On the other hand, most school systems in the past have avoided or given only lip service to the issue of parenting and parenting skills. The moral issue of illegitimate births aside, the reality of the world is that each year there are large numbers of children born to unwed parents who have had little, or no, training in child rearing.

What was done on the farm in the past is irrelevant here: the farm is gone and/or has been replaced by the inner city, and the pressing issue is how to train uneducated new parents in the child rearing tasks before them. Other issues are secondary to the immediate needs of newborns and their futures. And it is in their futures that the quality of life for all of us is found.

Thus, while we can debate this issue all we wish, we cannot responsibly ignore that uneducated parents need to be educated in the tasks before them, and it is clear that the best way to do this is in the school system, where these new parents are already learning how to be responsible citizens in the civics and other classes currently in place.

Notice how the writer moves sequentially from one idea to the next, maintaining throughout the parallel of citizenship and parenthood, from the opening quotation, paragraph by paragraph to the concluding sentence. Each idea is developed from the preceding idea, and each new idea refers to the preceding ideas, and at no point do related, but irrelevant issues sidetrack the writer.

COMPETENCY 11.0   UNDERSTAND THE APPLICATION OF WRITING SKILLS TO CLASSROOM INSTRUCTION

Skill 11.1   Demonstrate an awareness of techniques for helping students generate and organize ideas for writing (e.g., outlines, freewriting, graphic organizers)

Prewriting may include clustering, listing, brainstorming, mapping, free writing, and charting. Providing many ways for a student to develop ideas on a topic will increase his/her chances for success.

Remind students that as they prewrite they need to consider their audience. Prewriting strategies assist students in a variety of ways. Listed below are the most common prewriting strategies students can use to explore, plan and write on a topic. It is important to remember when teaching these strategies that not all prewriting must eventually produce a finished piece of writing. In fact, in the initial lesson of teaching prewriting strategies, it might be more effective to have students practice prewriting strategies without the pressure of having to write a finished product.

- Keep an idea book so that they can jot down ideas that come to mind
- Write in a daily journal
- Write down whatever comes to mind; this is called free writing. Students do not stop to make corrections or interrupt the flow of ideas.

A variation of this technique is focused free writing - writing on a specific topic - to prepare for an essay.

- Make a list of all ideas connected with their topic; this is called brainstorming
- Make sure students know that this technique works best when they let their mind work freely. After completing the list, students should analyze the list to see if a pattern or way to group the ideas
- Ask the questions Who? What? When? Where? When? and How? Help the writer approach a topic from several perspectives
- Create a visual map on paper to gather ideas. Cluster circles and lines to show connections between ideas. Students should try to identify the relationship that exists between their ideas. If they cannot see the relationships, have them pair up, exchange papers and have their partners look for some related ideas
- Observe details of sight, hearing, taste, touch, and taste
- Visualize by making mental images of something and write down the details in a list

Brainstorming

When brainstorming, quickly create a list of words and ideas that are connected to the topic. Let your mind roam free to generate as many relevant ideas as possible in a few minutes. For example, on the topic of computers you may write

computer- modern invention
types- personal computers, micro-chips in calculators and watches
wonder - acts like an electronic brain
uses - science, medicine, offices, homes, schools
problems- too much reliance; the machines aren't perfect

This list could help you focus on the topic and states the points you could develop in the body paragraphs. The brainstorming list keeps you on track and is well worth the few minutes it takes to jot down the ideas. While you haven't ordered the ideas, seeing them on paper is an important step.

Questioning

Questioning helps you focus as you mentally ask a series of exploratory questions about the topic. You may use the most basic questions: **who, what, where, when, why, and how.**

"What is my subject? "
[computers]

"What types of computers are there?"
[personal computers, micro-chip computers]

"Why have computers been a positive invention?"
[acts like an electronic brain in machinery and equipment; helps solve complex scientific problems]

"How have computers been a positive invention?"
[used to make improvements in:
- science (space exploration, moon landings)
- medicine (MRIs, CAT scans, surgical tools, research models)
- business (PCs, FAX, telephone equipment)
- education (computer programs for math, languages, science, social studies), and
- personal use (family budgets, **tax** programs, healthy diet plans)]

"How can I show that computers are good?"
[citing numerous examples]

"What problems do I see with computers?"
[too much reliance; not yet perfect.]

"**What** personal experiences would help me develop examples to respond to this topic?

    [my own experiences using computers]

Of course, you may not have time to write out the questions completely. You might just write the words *who, what, where, why, how* and the major points next to each. An abbreviated list might look as follows:

What — computers/modern wonder/making life better
How — through technological improvements: lasers, calculators, CAT scans, MRIs.

Where – in science and space exploration, medicine, schools, offices

In a few moments, your questions should help you to focus on the topic and to generate interesting ideas and points to make in the essay. Later in the writing process, you can look back at the list to be sure you've made the key points you intended.

Clustering

Some visual thinkers find clustering an effective prewriting method. When clustering, you draw a box in the center of your paper and write your topic within that box. Then you draw lines from the center box and connect it to small satellite boxes that contain related ideas. Here are some examples of visual organizers:

VISUAL ORGANIZER: GIVING REASONS

VISUAL ORGANIZER: GIVING INFORMATION

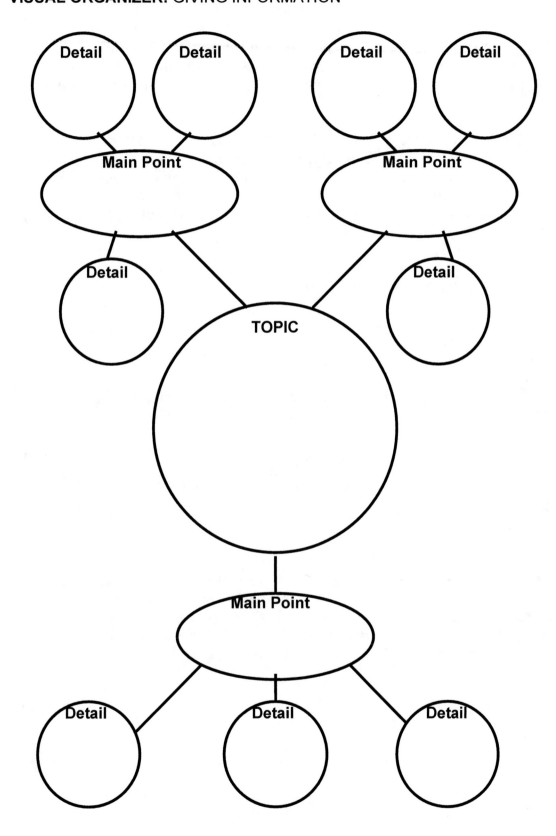

Creating a working outline

A good thesis gives structure to your essay and helps focus your thoughts. When forming your thesis, look at your prewriting strategy – clustering, questioning, or brainstorming. Then decide quickly which two or three major areas you'll discuss. Remember you must limit *the scope* of the paper because of the time factor.

The **outline** lists those main areas or points as topics for each paragraph. Looking at the prewriting cluster on computers, you might choose several areas in which computers help us, for example in science and medicine, business, and education. You might also consider people's reliance on this "wonder" and include at least one paragraph about this reliance. A formal outline for this essay might look like the one below:

I.   Introduction and thesis
II. Computers used in science and medicine
II. Computers used in business
IV. Computers used in education
V. People's reliance on computers
VI. Conclusion

Under time pressure, however, you may use a shorter organizational plan, such as abbreviated key words in a list. For example

1. intro: wonders of the computer OR
2. science
3. med
4. schools
5. business
6. conclusion

a. intro: wonders of computers - science
b. in the space industry
c. in medical technology
d. conclusion

After students have practiced with each of these prewriting strategies, ask them to pick out the ones they prefer and ask them to discuss how they might use the techniques to help them with future writing assignments. It is important to remember that they can use more than one prewriting strategy at a time. Also they may find that different writing situations may suggest certain techniques.

Skill 11.2 Demonstrate knowledge of methods for monitoring student writing and identify basic problems students may be having in their written work

Viewing writing as a process allows teachers and students to see the writing classroom as a cooperative workshop where students and teachers encourage and support each other in each writing endeavor. Listed below are some techniques that help teachers to facilitate and create a supportive classroom environment.

1. Create peer response/support groups that are working on similar writing assignments. The members help each other in all stages of the writing process-from prewriting, writing, revising, editing, and publishing.

2. Provide several prompts to give students the freedom to write on a topic of their own. Writing should be generated out of personal experience and students should be introduced to in-class journals. One effective way to get into writing is to let them write often and freely about their own lives, without having to worry about grades or evaluation.

3. Respond in the form of a question whenever possible. Teacher/facilitator should respond noncritically and use positive, supportive language.

4. Respond to formal writing acknowledging the student's strengths and focusing on the composition skills demonstrated by the writing. A response should encourage the student by offering praise for what the student has done well. Give the student a focus for revision and demonstrate that the process of revision has applications in many other writing situations.

5. Provide students with readers' checklists so that students can write observational critiques of others' drafts, and then they can revise their own papers at home using the checklists as a guide.

6. Pair students so that they can give and receive responses. Pairing students keeps them aware of the role of an audience in the composing process and in evaluating stylistic effects.

7. Focus critical comments on aspects of the writing that can be observed in the writing. Comments like "I noticed you use the word 'is' frequently" will be more helpful than "Your introduction is dull" and will not demoralize the writer.

8. Provide the group with a series of questions to guide them through the group writing sessions.

Skill 11.3   Recognize effective techniques for helping students edit and proofread their writing (e.g., correcting errors in grammar and spelling)

Revision is probably the most important step for the writer in the writing process. Here, students examine their work and make changes in wording, details and ideas. So many times, students write a draft and then feel they're done. On the contrary – students must be encouraged to develop, change, and enhance their writing as they go, as well as once they've completed a draft.

Many teachers introduce Writer's Workshop to their students to maximize learning about the writing process. Writer's Workshops vary across classrooms, but the main idea is for students to become comfortable with the writing process to produce written work. A basic Writer's Workshop will include a block of classroom time committed to writing various projects (i.e., narratives, memoirs, book summaries, fiction, book reports, etc). Students use this time to write, meet with others to review/edit writing, make comments on writing, revise their own work, proofread, meet with the teacher, and publish their work.

Teachers who facilitate effective Writer's Workshops are able to meet with students one at a time and can guide that student in their individual writing needs. This approach allows the teacher to differentiate instruction for each students' writing level. Viewing writing as a process allows teachers and students to see the writing classroom as a cooperative place where students and teachers encourage and support each other in each writing endeavor. Listed below are some techniques that help teachers to facilitate and create a supportive classroom environment.

When assessing and responding to student writing, there are several guidelines to remember.

Responding to non-graded writing (formative).

1. Avoid using a red pen. Whenever possible use a #2 pencil.
2. Explain the criteria that will be used for assessment in advance.
3. Read the writing once while asking the question, "Is the student's response appropriate for the assignment?"
4. Reread and make note at the end whether the student met the objective of the writing task.
5. Responses should be non-critical and use supportive and encouraging language.
6. Resist writing on or over the student's writing.
7. Highlight the ideas you wish to emphasize, question, or verify.
8. Encourage your students to take risks.

Responding to and evaluating graded writing (summative)

1. Ask students to submit prewriting and rough-draft materials including all revisions with their final draft.
2. For the first reading, use a holistic method, examining the work as a whole.
3. When reading the draft for the second time, assess it using the standards previously established.
4. Responses to the writing should be written in the margin and should use supportive language.
5. Make sure you address the process as well as the product. It is important that students value the learning process as well as the final product.
6. After scanning the piece a third time, write final comments at the end of the draft.

Skill 11.4   Demonstrate the ability to identify appropriate reference materials (e.g., dictionaries, library resources, the Internet) as well as effective techniques for helping students use them

In our increasingly knowledge-based world, educators have found that it is not good enough to simply teach students factual information. The information teachers pass on to students is inherently going to be limited and soon out-dated. It is said that the body of knowledge in most academic fields doubles within a matter of years. That being said, we can assume that the factual information students do get in the classroom will not necessarily represent the most current, accurate information available.

Because of the rapidly accelerating amount of information available, educators cannot shirk the responsibility of not teaching students how to access sources of information. References sources can be of great value, and by teaching students how to access these first, they will later have skills that will help them access more in-depth databases and sources of information.

Encyclopedias are reference materials that appear in book or electronic form. Encyclopedias can be considered general or specific. General encyclopedias peripherally cover most fields of knowledge; specific encyclopedias cover a smaller amount of material in greater depth. Encyclopedias are good first sources of information for students. While their total scope is limited, they can provide a quick introduction to topics so that students can get familiar with the topics before exploring the topics in greater depth.

Almanacs provide statistical information on various topics. Typically, these references are rather specific. They often cover a specific period of time. One famous example is the *Farmer's Almanac*. This annual publication summarizes, among many other things, weather conditions for the previous year.

Bibliographies contain references for further research. Bibliographies are usually organized topically. They help point people to the in-depth resources they will need for a complete view of a topic.

Databases, typically all electronic now, are collections of material on specific topics. For example, teachers can go online and find many databases of science articles for students in a variety of topics.

Atlases are visual representations of geographic areas. Often, they serve different functions. Some atlases demonstrate geologic attributes, while others emphasize populations of various areas.

Finally, **periodical guides** categorize articles and special editions of journals and magazines to help archive and organize the vast amount of material that is put in periodicals each year.

In all, reference tools are highly valuable for students. Surprisingly, it takes a very long time for students to become competent with most reference tools, but the effort and time is definitely worth it.

Dictionaries are useful for spelling, writing, and reading. It is very important to initially expose and habituate students to enjoy using the dictionary. Cooper (2004) suggests that the following be kept in mind as the teacher of grades K-6 introduces and then habituates children in what is to be hoped, will be a lifelong fascination with the dictionary and vocabulary acquisition.

Requesting or suggesting that children look up a word in the dictionary should be an invitation to a wonderful exploration, not a punishment or busy work that has no reference to their current reading assignment.

Model the correct way to use the dictionary for children even as late as the third – sixth grade. Many have never been taught proper dictionary skills. The teacher needs to demonstrate to the children that as an adult reader and writer, he or she, routinely and happily uses the dictionary and learns new stuff that makes him or her better at reading and writing.

Do not routinely require children to look up every new spelling word in the dictionary

Some experts believe in beginning dictionary study as early as kindergarten and this is now very possible because of the proliferation of lush picture dictionaries which can be introduced at that grade level. These experts also suggest that children not only look at these picture dictionaries, but also begin to make dictionaries of their own at this grade level filled with pictures and beginning words. As children join the circle of lexicographers, they will begin to see themselves, as compilers and users of dictionaries. Of course, this will support their ongoing vocabulary development.

On early grade levels, use of the dictionary can nicely complement the c
mastery of the alphabet. They should be given whole class and small
practice in locating words.

As the children progress with their phonetic skills, the dictionary ca
show them phonetic respelling using the pronunciation key.

Older children in grades 3 and beyond need explicit teacher demor
practice in use of guide words. They also need to begin to learn ab
hierarchies of various word meanings. In the upper grades, children
explore using special content dictionaries and glossaries in the backs c
books.

Primary and secondary sources

The resources used to support a piece of writing can be divided into two major
groups: primary sources and secondary sources.

Primary sources are works, records, etc. that were created during the period
being studied or immediately after it. Secondary sources are works written
significantly after the period being studied and based upon primary sources.
Primary sources are the basic materials that provide raw data and information.
Secondary sources are the works that contain the explications of, and judgments
on, this primary material.

Primary sources include the following kinds of materials:

- Documents that reflect the immediate, everyday concerns of people:
  memoranda, bills, deeds, charters, newspaper reports, pamphlets, graffiti,
  popular writings, journals or diaries, records of decision-making bodies,
  letters, receipts, snapshots.
- Theoretical writings which reflect care and consideration in composition
  and an attempt to convince or persuade. The topic will generally be
  deeper and more pervasive values than is the case with "immediate"
  documents. These may include newspaper or magazine editorials,
  sermons, political speeches, philosophical writings.
- Narrative accounts of events, ideas, and trends written with intentionality
  by someone contemporary with the events described.
- Statistical data, although statistics may be misleading.
- Literature and nonverbal materials, novels, stories, poetry and essays
  from the period, as well as coins, archaeological artifacts, and art
  produced during the period.

Guidelines for the use of primary resources:

1. Be certain that you understand how language was used at the time of writing and that you understand the context in which it was produced.
2. Do not read history blindly; but be certain that you understand both explicit and implicit referenced in the material.
3. Read the entire text you are reviewing; do not simply extract a few sentences to read.
4. Although anthologies of materials may help you identify primary source materials, the full original text should be consulted.

Secondary sources include the following kinds of materials:

- Books written on the basis of primary materials about the period of time.
- Books written on the basis of primary materials about persons who played a major role in the events under consideration.
- Books and articles written on the basis of primary materials about the culture, the social norms, the language, and the values of the period.
- Quotations from primary sources.
- Statistical data on the period.
- The conclusions and inferences of other historians.
- Multiple interpretations of the ethos of the time.

Guidelines for the use of secondary sources:

1. Do not rely upon only a single secondary source.
2. Check facts and interpretations against primary sources whenever possible.
3. Do not accept the conclusions of other historians uncritically.
4. Place greatest reliance on secondary sources created by the best and most respected scholars.
5. Do not use the inferences of other scholars as if they were facts.
6. Ensure that you recognize any bias the writer brings to his/her interpretation of history.
7. Understand the primary point of the book as a basis for evaluating the value of the material presented in it to your questions.

Selects and uses instructional strategies, materials, and activities to help children use multiple sources, including electronic texts, experts, and print resources, to locate information

Locating information for research projects and compiling research sources using both print and electronic resources is vital in the construct of written documents. The resources that are available in today's school communities include a large database of Internet resources and World Wide Web access that provides individual navigation for print and electronic information. Research sources include looking at traditional commercial databases and using The Electronic Library to print and cite a diversity of informational resources.

The vital aspect of the research process includes learning to analyze the applicability and validity of the massive amounts of accessible information in cyberspace. Verifying and evaluating electronic resources are part of the process of sorting through the downloaded hardcopies or scrolling through the electronic databases. In using a diversity of research sources, the user must be able to discern authentic sources of information from the mass collections of websites and information databases.

In primary research, selecting a topic and setting up an outline for research information precedes using the secondary research of both print and electronic resources. Using conceptual Venn diagrams to center the topic and brainstorm the peripheral information pertaining to the topic clarifies the purpose of the research. There are two aspects of the secondary research: one, using print sources and two, using electronic research tools.

Print sources provide guides on locations for specific or general information resources. Libraries have floors or designated areas dedicated to the collection of encyclopedias, specific resource manuals, card catalogs, and periodical indexes that will provide information on the projected topic. Electronic research tools includes a listing of the latest and most effective search engines like Goggle, Microsoft, AOL, Infotrac and Yahoo to find the topic of research, along with peripheral support information. Electronic databases that contain extensive resources will provide the user with selecting resources, choosing effective keywords, and constructing search strategies. The world of electronic research opens up a global library of resources for both print and electronic information.

The major online services such as Microsoft, Prodigy, and CompuServe provide users with assess information of specialized information that is either free or one that has a minimal charge assessed for that specific service or website. Online resources teach effective ways to bookmark sites of interest and how to cut and paste relevant information onto word documents for citation and reference.

Bookmarking favorite Internet searches that contain correct sources for reference can save a lot of research time. On AOL, book marking is known as favorites and with one click of the mouse, a user can type in the email address on the browser's location bar and create instant access to that location. Netscape uses the terminology of "bookmarks" to save browser locations for future research.

Online search engines and web portals create avenues of navigating the World Wide Web Web portals provide linkages to other websites and are typically subdivided into other categories for searching. Portals are also specific to certain audience interests that index parts of the web. Search engines can provide additional strategic site searches.

COMPETENCY 12.0 UNDERSTAND APPLICATION OF MATHEMATICS SKILLS TO CLASSROOM INSTRUCTION

Skill 12.1 Demonstrate the ability to relate mathematics to everyday situations

See Competencies 7.0 and 8.0.

Skill 12.2 Identify and correcting basic errors in addition, subtraction, multiplication, and division

The following are some possible types of errors in mathematical explanations:

- Information not appropriate or extraneous to the explanation
- Misuse of mathematical terms
- Inappropriate strategy for solving the problem
- Inappropriate or unexplained diagram
- Incomplete argument
- Incorrect labels or descriptions
- Key elements of the strategy are missing
- Algorithms incorrectly executed
- Words do not reflect the problem
- Process cannot be identified

See also Skill 7.1.

Skill 12.3 Demonstrate knowledge of techniques for helping students use instructional resources (e.g., math manipulative materials, rulers, money, charts, graphs, calculators) to support mathematical learning

Successful math teachers introduce their students to multiple problem solving strategies and create a classroom environment where free thought and experimentation are encouraged. Teachers can promote problem solving by allowing multiple attempts at problems, giving credit for reworking test or homework problems, and encouraging the sharing of ideas through class discussion. There are several specific problem solving skills with which teachers should be familiar.

The **guess-and-check** strategy calls for students to make an initial guess at the solution, check the answer, and use the outcome of to guide the next guess. With each successive guess, the student should get closer to the correct answer. Constructing a table from the guesses can help organize the data.

Example: There are 100 coins in a jar. 10 are dimes. The rest are pennies and nickels. There are twice as many pennies as nickels. How many pennies and nickels are in the jar?

There are 90 total nickels and pennies in the jar (100 coins – 10 dimes).

There are twice as many pennies as nickels. Make guesses that fulfill the criteria and adjust based on the answer found. Continue until we find the correct answer, 60 pennies and 30 nickels.

Number of Pennies	Number of Nickels	Total Number of Pennies and Nickels
40	20	60
80	40	120
70	35	105
60	30	90

When solving a problem where the final result and the steps to reach the result are given, students must **work backwards** to determine what the starting point must have been.

Example: John subtracted seven from his age, and divided the result by 3. The final result was 4. What is John's age?

Work backward by reversing the operations.
4 x 3 = 12;
12 + 7 = 19
John is 19 years old.

Drawing pictures or diagrams can sometimes help to make relationships in a problem clearer.

For example: In a women's marathon, the first five finishers in some order were Freida, Polly, Christa, Betty, and Dora. Freida finished seven seconds before Christa. Polly finished six seconds after Betty. Dora finished eight seconds after Betty. Christa finished two seconds before Polly. In what order did the women finish the race?

Drawing a picture or diagram will help us see the answer easily.

From the diagram, we can see that the women finished in the following order: 1st – Freida, 2nd – Betty, 3rd – Christa, 4th – Polly, and 5th – Dora.

Sometimes, using a model is the best way to see the solution to a problem, as in the case of fraction multiplication.

For example: Model $\dfrac{5}{6} \times \dfrac{2}{3}$.

Draw a rectangle. Divide it vertically into 6 equal sections (the denominator of the first number.)

Divide the rectangle horizontally into 3 equal sections (the denominator of the second number).

Color in a number of vertical strips equal to the numerator of the first number.

Use a different color to shade a number of horizontal strips equal to the numerator of the second number.

By describing the area where both colors overlap, we have the product of the two fractions -- $\dfrac{10}{18}$.

Sample Test: Instructional Support

1. **The major difference between phonemic and phonological awareness is:**

   A. One deals with a series of discrete sounds and sound spelling relationships.
   B. One is involved with teaching and learning alliteration and rhymes.
   C. Phonemic awareness is a specific type phonological awareness that deals with separate phonemes within a given word.
   D. Phonological awareness is associated with printed words.

2. **All of the following are true about phonological awareness EXCEPT:**

   A. It may involve print.
   B. It is a prerequisite for spelling and phonics.
   C. Activities can be done by the children with their eyes closed.
   D. Starts before letter recognition is taught.

3. **Julia has been hired to work in a school that serves a local public housing project. She is working with kindergarten children and has been asked to focus on shared reading. She selects:**

   A. Chapter books.
   B. Riddle books.
   C. Alphabet books.
   D. Wordless picture books.

4. **A teacher has taught his students several strategies to monitor their reading comprehension. These strategies include identifying where in the passage they are having difficulty, identifying what the difficulty is, and restating the difficult sentence or passage in their own words. These strategies are examples of:**

   A. graphic and semantic organizers
   B. metacognition
   C. recognizing story structure
   D. summarizing

5. **Varying the complexity of a graphic organizer would be an example of differentiating:**

   A. content/topic
   B. environment
   C. process
   D. product

6. **The best way for a primary grade teacher to model directionality and one to one word matching would be:**

   A. Using a regular library or classroom text book.
   B. Using her own person reading book.
   C. Using a big book.
   D. Using a book dummy.

7. **To decode is to:**

   A. Construct meaning.
   B. Sound out a printed sequence of letters.
   C. Use a special code to decipher a message.
   D. None of the above.

8. **Asking a child if what he or she has read makes sense to him or her, is prompting the child to use:**

   A. Phonics cues.
   B. Syntactic cues.
   C. Semantic cues.
   D. Prior knowledge.

9. **When you ask a child, if what he or she has just read "sounds right" to him or her, you are trying to get that child to use:**

   A. Phonics cues.
   B. Syntactic cues.
   C. Semantic cues.
   D. Prior knowledge.

10. **The word "bat" is a ___word for "batter-up":**

    A. Suffix.
    B. Prefix.
    C. Root word.
    D. Inflectional ending.

11. **As part of study about the agricultural products of their state, children have identified 22 different types of apples produced in the state. They can use a _____to compare and contrast these different types of apples:**

    A. Word web.
    B. Semantic map.
    C. Semantic features analysis grid.
    D. All of the above.

12. **To help children with "main idea" questions, the teacher should:**

    A. Give out a strategy sheet on the main idea for children to place in their reader's notebooks.
    B. Model responding to such a question as part of the guided reading.
    C. Have children create "main idea questions" to go with their writings.
    D. All of the above.

13. **"Self correct" in reading means:**

    A. The teacher corrects on the record the errors the child makes.
    B. The child goes back and corrects errors made in a running record.
    C. The reading specialist teaches this to the child.
    D. a and b.

14. **Making inferences from the text means that the reader:**

    A. Is making informed judgments based on available evidence.
    B. Is making a guess based on prior experiences.
    C. Is making a guess based on what the reader would like to be true of the text.
    D. All of the above.

15. **Sometimes children can be asked to demonstrate their understanding of a text in a non-written format. This might include all of the following except:**

    A. A story map.
    B. A Venn diagram.
    C. Storyboarding a part of the story with dialogue bubbles.
    D. Retelling or paraphrasing.

16. **How could a KWL chart be used in instruction?**

    A. To motivate students to do a research paper
    B. To assess prior knowledge of the students
    C. To assist in teaching skills
    D. To put events in sequential order

17. **Which of the following is considered a study skill?**

    A. Using graphs, tables, and maps
    B. Using a desk-top publishing program
    C. Explaining important vocabulary words
    D. Asking for clarification

18. **A sixth-grade science teacher has given her class a paper to read on the relationship between food and weight gain. The writing contains signal words such as "because," "consequently," "this is how," and "due to." This paper has which text structure?**

    A. cause & effect
    B. compare & contrast
    C. description
    D. sequencing

19. A student has written a paper with the following characteristics: written in first person; characters, setting, and plot; some dialogue; events organized in chronological sequence with some flashbacks. In what genre has the student written?

A. expository writing
B. narrative writing
C. persuasive writing
D. technical writing

20. If a student uses inappropriate language that includes slang and expletives, what is the best course of action to take in order to influence the student's formal communication skills?

A. Ask the student to paraphrase the writing, that is, translate it into language appropriate for the school principal to read.
B. Refuse to read the student's papers until he conforms to a more literate style.
C. Ask the student to read his work aloud to the class for peer evaluation.
D. Rewrite the flagrant passages to show the student the right form of expression.

21. Of the following, which one is the Middle-School student most likely to be encountering for the first time?

A. Phonics.
B. Phonemics.
C. Textbook reading assignments.
D. Stories read by the teacher.

22. The practice of reading a piece of student writing to assess the overall impression of the product is:

A. holistic evaluation.
B. portfolio assessment.
C. analytical evaluation.
D. using a performance system.

23. A technique used to allow students to present written ideas without interruption of the flow of thoughts is called:

A. brainstorming.
B. mapping.
C. listing.
D. Free writing.

24. Which of the following is not a technique of prewriting?

A. Clustering
B. Listing
C. Brainstorming
D. Proofreading

25. **Which of the following is the least preferable strategy for teaching literature?**

   A. Teacher-guided total class discussion
   B. Small group discussion
   C. Teacher lecture
   D. Dramatization of literature selections

Answer Key: Instructional Support

1.	C		14.	A
2.	A		15.	D
3.	D		16.	B
4.	C		17.	A.
5.	C		18.	A
6.	C		19.	B
7.	B		20.	A
8.	C		21.	C
9.	B		22.	A
10.	C		23.	D
11.	D		24.	D
12.	D		25.	C
13.	B			

Rationales for Sample Questions: Instructional Support

1. This is a sheer memorization question. By definition, phonemic awareness falls under the phonological awareness umbrella. All of the other choices do not deal with the DIFFERENCE between the two types of awareness.

2. The key word here is EXCEPT which will be highlighted in upper case on the test as well. All of the options are correct aspects of phonological awareness except the first one, A, because phonological awareness DOES NOT involve print.

3. Given the fact this is a kindergarten in a public housing project, she will be most successful with wordless picture books, since there is no guarantee the children have had prior exposure to the other types of books listed. The answer "D" will allow them to construct a story from the pictures.

4. The correct answer is C. Metacognition may be defined as "thinking about thinking." Good readers use metacognitive strategies to think about and have control over their reading. Before reading, they might clarify their purpose for reading and preview the text. During reading, they might monitor their understanding, adjusting their reading speed to fit the difficulty of the text and fixing any comprehension problems they have. After reading, they check their understanding of what they read.

5. The correct answer is C. Differentiating the processes means varying learning activities or strategies to provide appropriate methods for students to explore the concepts. It is important to give students alternative paths to manipulate the ideas embedded within the concept. For example, students may use graphic organizers, maps, diagrams, or charts to display their comprehension of concepts covered. Varying the complexity of the graphic organizer can very effectively facilitate differing levels of cognitive processing for students of differing ability.

6. Key word in this question is "best" and the answer is "C" because this type of a book is best for teaching and display.

7. The answer is "B."

8. Semantic cues are the hints that students can discern from the reading to help them make sense of the text. In some cases, the message of the text depends on the other words around them, so students learn how to determine the meaning from context clues. The answer must be "C."

9. This is another one of those 'scripted" answers currently in use in reading. The answer has to be "B," syntactic clues.

10. The answer is "C."

11. The answer here is "D" and all of these graphic organizers would work with the apples.

12. This is one where all the options are right. The answer is "D."

13. There is only one correct answer here and it is "B." This is a key principle of the running record and of keeping any reading record.

14. This is a definition question that a literate test taker can answer based on the general definition of inferences. The answer is "A."

15. Answer "D" is correct. Retelling and paraphrasing can be in oral form whereas the other choices all involve writing or the use of pencil and paper. By asking students to retell a story, the teacher can determine the level of comprehension. Of course, this has to be modeled for the student, especially paraphrasing, so that the student relates the important facts or events and does not include any information that is not necessary.

16. B. To understand information, not simply repeat it, students must connect it to their previous understanding. Textbooks can't do that. Instead, teachers—the people who know students best—have to find out what they know and how to build on that knowledge. In science, having students make predictions before conducting experiments is an obvious way of finding out what they know, and having them compare their observations to those predictions helps connect new knowledge and old. In history, teachers can also ask students what they know about a topic before they begin studying it or ask them to make predictions about what they will learn. KWL charts, in which students discuss what they know, what they want to know, and (later) what they have learned, are one way to activate this prior knowledge.

17. In studying, it is certainly true that "a picture is worth a thousand words." Not only are these devices useful in making a point clear, they are excellent mnemonic devices for remembering facts. The answer is "A."

18. The answer is A. Cause and effect is the relationship between two things when one thing makes something else happen. Writers use this text structure to show order, inform, speculate, and change behavior. This text structure uses the process of identifying potential causes of a problem or issue in an orderly way. It is often used to teach social studies and science concepts. It is characterized by signal words such as because, so, so that, if... then, consequently, thus, since, for, for this reason, as a result of, therefore, due to, this is how, nevertheless, and accordingly.

19. The correct answer is B. These are all characteristics of narrative writing. Expository writing is intended to give information such as an explanation or directions, and the information is logically organized. Persuasive writing gives an opinion in an attempt to convince the reader that this point of view is valid or tries to persuade the reader to take a specific action. The goal of technical writing is to clearly communicate a select piece of information to a targeted reader or group of readers for a particular purpose in such a way that the subject can readily be understood. It is persuasive writing that anticipates a response from the reader.

20. The answer is A. Asking the student to write for a specific audience will help him become more involved in his writing. If he continues writing to the same audience—the teacher—he will continue seeing writing as just another assignment and he will not apply grammar, vocabulary, and syntax the way they should be. By paraphrasing his own writing, the student will learn to write for a different public.

21. The correct answer is C. For the first time, the student will be expected to read textbook assignments and come to class prepared to discuss the content.

22. The answer is A. Holistic Scoring assesses a piece of writing as a whole. Usually a paper is read quickly through once to get a general impression. The writing is graded according to the impression of the whole work rather than the sum of its parts. Often holistic scoring uses a rubric that establishes the overall criteria for a certain score to evaluate each paper.

23. The answer is D. Free writing fourteen or fifteen minutes allows the student to write out his/her thoughts about a subject. This technique allows the student to develop ideas s/he is conscious of, but it also helps him/her develop ideas that belong to the subconscious. It is important to let the flow of ideas run through the hand. If the student gets stuck, s/he can write the last sentence over again until inspiration comes back.

24. The answer is D. Proofreading should be reserved for the final draft.

25. The answer is C. In order to engage students' interest, it is necessary that they be involved whether through discussion or dramatization. A lecture is a much too passive technique to involve students of this age.

XAMonline, INC. 21 Orient Ave. Melrose, MA 02176

Toll Free number 800-509-4128

TO ORDER Fax 781-662-9268 OR www.XAMonline.com

GEORGIA ASSESSMENTS FOR THE CERTIFICATION OF EDUCATORS   -GACE - 2007

PO#   Store/School:

Address 1:

Address 2 (Ship to other):

City, State Zip

Credit card number_____-_____-_____-_____   expiration_____

EMAIL _____

PHONE   **FAX**

13# ISBN 2007	TITLE	Qty	Retail	Total
978-1-58197-533-8	Basic Skills 200, 201, 202			
978-1-58197-528-4	Biology 026, 027			
978-1-58197-529-1	Science 024, 025			
978-1-58197-532-1	Physics Sample Test 030, 031			
978-1-58197-531-4	Art Education Sample Test 109, 110			
978-1-58197-574-1	English 020, 021			
978-1-58197-545-1	History 034, 035			
978-1-58197-527-7	Health and Physical Education 115, 116			
978-1-58197-540-6	Chemistry 028, 029			
978-1-58197-534-5	Reading 117, 118			
978-1-58197-547-5	Media Specialist 101, 102			
978-1-58197-573-4	Middle Grades Language Arts 011			
978-1-58197-535-2	Middle Grades Reading 012			
978-1-58197-539-0	Middle Grades Science 014			
978-1-58197-543-7	Middle Grades Mathematics 013			
978-1-58197-546-8	Middle Grades Social Science 015			
978-1-58197-536-9	Mathematics 022, 023			
978-1-58197-549-9	Political Science 032, 033			
978-1-58197-544-4	Paraprofessional Assessment 177			
978-1-58197-542-0	Professional Pedagogy Assessment 171, 172			
978-1-58197-537-6	Early Childhood Education 001, 002			
978-1-58197-548-2	School Counseling 103, 104			
978-1-58197-541-3	Spanish 141, 142			
978-1-58197-538-3	Special Education General Curriculum 081, 082			
978-1-58197-530-7	French Sample Test 143, 144			

	SUBTOTAL	
FOR PRODUCT PRICES GO TO WWW.XAMONLINE.COM	Ship	$8.25
	TOTAL	